P9-DWE-145

Carl
AKERS'
COLORADO

Carl AKERS' COLORADO

THE OLD ARMY PRESS

Photographs courtesy of the
Denver Public Library,
Western History Department

Color photography by Carl Akers
and Frank Currier

Research by Margaret Akers

1513 Welch
Fort Collins, Colorado 80521

Contents

Introduction

This book is the partial result of many hours during more than 25-years of pouring through countless old books and papers and diaries . . . some sneezingly musty . . . and piloting a bouncing four-wheel-drive over high-country trails; 25-years of fascination with Colorado and everything in it, and of those incredibly tough characters who first came here, took on the wilderness and its dangers . . . and left us a most beautiful place to live.

The history of Colorado doesn't seem like history. It is so recent that you can touch it and feel it and, sometimes, even hear it. It requires very little imagination.

The text of this book is selected parts of nearly a dozen scripts which were written for television specials. The stories are about only a few old towns; we couldn't cover them all . . . since each community in the state has its own stories. The text is written to be read aloud, or to yourself as you want of course. Whichever way, we sincerely hope you enjoy it . . . since all the effort which has gone into it really hasn't seemed like much effort at all.

Leadville

"It was something else again,
this place . . . and it still is."

11

In early 1860, the settlement called Denver . . . jam-up next to the Front Range . . . was only a little more than a year old. It was the cross-roads of hundreds and thousands of get-rich-quickers pouring across the plains from the east . . . and hundreds and thousands of others . . . tired, angry and disappointed . . . trudging back across those same, dangerous plains toward home. The Shining Mountains weren't solid gold after all . . . and the country was hard and demanding and unforgiving. So, many went back. But many stayed . . . thousands of them . . . and found what they wanted, the hard way.

By early 1860, Gregory Gulch had been ripped and torn for almost a year and, it seemed, the hills were, in fact solid gold. Others had wandered over the ridges and had found it along the Blue, and in South Park, and in other places. Still others pushed even deeper into those forbidding mountains.

One little band climbed into the upper valley of the Arkansas . . . and found another group already there, painfully picking a few grains of gold out of the bars at Cache Creek. Nobody paid much attention, except there was a woman with a baby living in one of the wagons . . . while her tall, raw-boned, tired-looking husband searched along the creek. He was a former Vermont stone-cutter, but that meant nothing; everybody out in this wild country came from someplace else . . . everybody looking for something better. So, the newly-arrived band pushed on . . . up the river . . . peering at each little stream that gurgled into the broad, grassy valley. They were disappointed . . . again; there was nothing here . . . and the seven started to move on.

But one of them . . . his name was Abe Lee . . . said he'd wash just one more pan . . . and did . . . and let out a yell that he had the whole state of California in his pan. And that yell echoed across all those ranges to the east . . .

And here they came, whooping and hollering, shirt-tails flying . . . gasping for breath up and down those high, barren ridges. Down the valley, that Vermont stone-cutter heard it and, once again, packed up his family, and whipped his ox-team to the place where the gold had been found. He told them his name was Tabor . . . Horace Tabor . . . and his wife's name was Augusta.

Augusta Tabor

"He was the first of the great Bonanza Kings . . ."

By that summer, there were five-thousand men in camp . . . tearing at that quiet little gulch . . . turning it into a happy, grinning disaster area. They chopped out a place in the pine-flats for a one-street town which they grandly named Oro City. And still they came . . . 10-thousand by the spring of '61. And the gold poured out of the gulch.

They ran ditches and wooden flumes down from the mountain to bring water for their sluice boxes.

They ran pipes to the gulch and gouged away at the banks with great streams of water under high-pressure . . . and the gold continued to flow . . . and the little valley, which they called California Gulch, was torn, re-torn and torn again.

There was trouble . . . a heavy, black sand that kept clogging their sluice boxes, and they roundly cussed it because it slowed down their unbridled ripping of the valley. They knew the black stuff wasn't gold, so it was worthless, of course; it was a nuisance . . . nothing more. And they cussed it.

So frantic was the digging that, in less than two years, the gulch seemingly had given all it had to give. And the thousands took what they had and climbed slowly back out of the valley. Horace Tabor had, like all the others, dug a few holes . . . but found nothing. He'd opened a store in Oro City, but Augusta had to run it . . . and patch up injured miners . . . and take care of their gold dust. The Tabors sadly watched the exodus and, finally, when only a few were left in the gulch, they loaded what they could carry and moved over the mountain like the rest. They stayed over there for six-years . . . running a store and a post office . . . until the elusive rainbow moved again . . . back toward California Gulch. And back they came . . . to set up another store in another Oro City which had been moved up to a spot in the gulch. It was as good a place as any other; a few men were still finding enough gold to keep it from dying. But, it was just a matter of time . . . and they knew it. That heavy black sand was still giving them trouble, and the few grains of gold they were finding were hardly worth the trouble. After 16-years, the little gulch had given up more than three-million-dollars and everything had to end sometime.

But then, in 1876, an old gold-miner, Uncle Billy Stevens, who was still grubbing in the gulch teamed up with a new-comer, A. B. Wood. They talked about and wondered about that black sand which was such a problem. They analyzed it and found it was something the experts called carbonate of lead . . . and it stunned them . . . it was loaded with silver . . . silver in a gold-mining area. They shook their heads in happy disbelief and quietly began looking for the source . . . and they found it . . . a surface vein on both sides of the mistreated little gulch. They were goggle-eyed, but quietly laid out their claims . . . and just as quietly began to dig . . . and nobody paid

them any mind. Everybody knew the gulch was just about worked out, so why bother. And nobody did . . . until, a year later, Wood startled everybody when he sold his half-interest to a business partner of Chicago's Marshal Field for 40-thousand dollars . . . 40-thousand-dollars . . . and that did it, again. And here they came again . . . not too many at first since an ounce of silver was worth only around one-twentieth as much as gold and took more work. But, then . . . 40-thousand dollars was a lot of money from a played-out gulch . . . and since it seemed that all the gold in Colorado had been found already, they might as well dig for silver. So they dug for silver. Three dirt-poor Gallagher Brothers quit their jobs in Uncle Billy's mine and wandered over to Strayhorse Gulch, picked a spot and started digging. They ran out of provisions, and had to go back to work to save enough money to work their claim again, then worked again, and quit again, and dug again . . . and hit a vein of almost solid silver.

Two sawmill hands, who worked long hard hours for just enough money to stay alive, climbed up among the trees on Iron Hill, dug . . . and took out 70-thousand-dollars in three months.

The stories flamed through the other camps in the mountains, and high, barren, dangerous Mosquito Pass was alive with men-with-money-wanting-more . . . and men-with-nothing-wanting-something . . . almost trampling each other to get to the fabulous new diggings, even though it was only silver.

And, every hole was lined with the stuff; all a man had to do was dig . . . and many didn't even do that. Bill Yankee laid out a claim, went into town and sold it for 50-thousand-dollars — and Yankee Hill boomed. George Fryer, who'd never been any closer to mining than running a lunch-counter over in Fairplay, picked a low hill just back of town and began to dig. The others laughed at him; said he was wasting his time; there was nothing on that hill. But, he went on digging, by himself, and uncovered something in excess of a million dollars . . . and named it the New Discovery. A lace-importer came out from the East, bought two gold claims in California Gulch, but hit silver instead . . . and laid the foundation of one of the nation's greatest fortunes. His name was Meyer Guggenheim.

Meyer Guggenheim

Down in New Oro City, Horace and Augusta Tabor watched all the frenetic activity . . . watched the inpouring of miners and teamsters and lumberjacks . . and businessmen and lawyers and gamblers . . . and preachers and engineers and ladies of all sorts . . . and every type of fast-buck, con-artist and criminal mind there was.

It had been too many years since there was a wide-open new camp like this; other camps had been worked out and disappeared, or had become towns and were

setting down to boring respectability. So, here it was . . . this bright new anything-goes-just-like-in-the-old-days camps . . . and anything did . . . night and day. And everybody wanted a piece of the action . . . and usually got it, one way or the other.

There was no rhyme-or-reason in the town; cabins and tents were scattered everywhere among what trees were left; wagons were parked wherever they happened to stop . . . with people living in them, and under them. Except for Chestnut and Harrison, there were no streets . . . only paths wandering around and through the slab-sided cabins.

Leadville 1879

“. . . and the silver kept pouring out of the ground.”

Huge tents held scores of two-tiered double-bunks that were occupied round-the-clock . . . 50-cents to a dollar for an eight-hour rest; when one man's time was up, another took his place. When the tents were full, the saloon-floors were packed with sleeping men . . . some of whom paid extra to be near the stove. Others slept wherever they could find a place out of the weather . . . even in wood bins and in out-houses . . . and hundreds of them died . . . either of pneumonia . . . or, simply, they froze to death. Many were buried at night so nobody would know the mounting death rate. There was one prospector who froze while working his claim; they set a charge of dynamite in the frozen ground to blast out a grave . . . and hit rich ore . . . and left him, forgotten in a snow-back, until the spring thaw.

Horace and Augusta Tabor watched it all . . . and ran their four-room, store-front, post-office-bar-hotel . . . and did quite well for themselves. Tabor was nearly 50; he was tired from chasing one will-o-the-wisp after another in the mountains for almost 20 years. He was doing all right, with Augusta's constant help; he gambled a little, ran the store sometimes; joined with a group to select a name for the new town . . . and, without much imagination but with a great deal of practicality . . . called it Leadville. And Tabor was named the first mayor and was a happy man . . . even though all that wealth flowing around him was going into other pockets.

Some of it was taken at gunpoint by gangs of thugs that terrorized the new town. On two occasions, they tried to tear down . . . to get the valuable lumber . . . the town's only hospital, but were driven off by armed vigilantes. Anything stealable was stolen. One temperance lecturer kept his Bible chained to the pulpit . . . which was bolted to the floor. A miner could leave his log-hut for work, and return to find every log, every board, every shingle and even the foundation gone.

Sawmills ran night and day turning out millions-of-feet of green lumber that quickly became drafty buildings of all sorts . . . and the hills for miles in every direction were stripped of their trees. Every second or third building was a gambling hall or a saloon or a crib or a parlor house . . . and there was a never-ending din . . . noise that ricocheted off the Mosquitoes to the east and towering Mount Elbert, the highest peak in the state, across the valley to the west.

And still they came . . . by the hundreds during that summer of 1878 . . . and even during the winter when the roads were all but impassable . . . when the temperature down in town hovered around zero for days at a time, and sometimes dropped to 30-to-40-below.

Despite everything, they kept on coming . . . most of them over that soaring pass that wasn't really a pass . . . just a slight depression in the treeless ridge.

They called it Mosquito Pass and it was, and still is, the highest traverse in North America . . . more than 13-thousand-feet at its summit. The newspaper said of Mosquito: "Here, a slip by one of the horses, a break in the harness, a mistake or even a slight hesitation on the part of the driver spells disaster." And the drivers drank a lot.

Mosquito Pass

During the second year of the boom, there were five stagecoach lines running constantly into and out of Leadville . . . and Mosquito Pass carried the heaviest traffic. It was the main route, a deeply-cut constantly-used route for 20-years . . . until the railroad finally came in 1880. So many men tried to walk the pass and so many of them died that it was called the "highway of frozen death".

But, those unbelievable holes-in-the-ground kept pouring forth incredible wealth . . . and still more discoveries were made. There was an Englishman, armed only with a pick and shovel, who wandered up one of the hills, stopped to ask a busy miner where to dig, was impatiently told . . . with a general swing of the arm . . . over there. And he walked over there . . . and dug . . . and hit the Little Jonny which made multi-millionaires out of its later owners.

Mayor Tabor probably shook his head . . . but, as mayor, had other duties . . . and, anyway, Augusta's store was doing very well, and they were contented. But, it didn't last. And no one had ever seen anything like it.

During that summer of 1878, there was an explosion . . . an explosion so incredible . . . it was heard throughout the nation. It started when two, down-at-the-heels grimy shoe-cobblers wandered over Mosquito into town. Their names, if anybody cared and nobody

"There must be lots of ghosts up there on those high, cold peaks . . ."

did . . . were August Rische and George Hook. They were just two of the hundreds who'd given up their trade in hopes of something better . . . nondescript, homeless and broke. The only thing they knew for sure about mining was . . . that mines are usually up on hills, nothing more. They shuffled into Tabor's store and asked for a grubstake, and were turned down; they came back again with the same request . . . and Tabor impatiently told them to take what they wanted, and go . . . and they did . . . 17-dollars worth of provisions which included a small jug of whiskey. And, since they knew that mines were usually on hills, they started climbing one. But it was a warm day and they sat down to rest in the shade of a tree . . . and sip at that jug. They discussed the situation and decided to dig . . . right there; it was as good a place as any . . . and, best of all, it was in the shade. So, they started digging and were down only 25-feet when they hit what looked like ore of some sort. It was . . one of the richest veins in the district . . . and they named it the Little Pittsburgh. Later, experts said if they'd dug 10-feet in any other direction, they'd probably have missed the vein . . . since nowhere in the district did the ore-body come that close to the surface . . . and it was practically solid silver. Because of that 17-dollar grubstake, Tabor got a third of the find and, within two months, began sharing 20-thousand-dollars-a-week. Hook decided it was too much for him; his partners, Tabor and Rische, paid him 100-thousand-dollars for his interest . . . and Rische turned around and sold his half of the mine to a group of bankers for 265-thousand-dollars . . . and Tabor was offered, and took, one-million-dollars for his half . . . and quickly made another million when the stock he'd kept soared from five to 30-dollars-a-share.

Within only a few months, he had skyrocketed from a store-keeper to a millionaire, twice-over. And the explosion wasn't finished yet, not by several more million. A sly old prospector, with the heart of a con-artist . . . Chicken Bill Lovell . . . went up Fryer Hill, dug a hole, salted it with ore stolen from Tabor's own mine . . . and sold it to the still-giddy Tabor for 40-thousand-dollars . . . and left town quickly. Tabor may have known that he'd been taken, since everybody else did, but he set crews to digging in the salted hole . . . and within three days, they'd hit the richest body of ore that had been found up to that time.

He named it the Chrysolite . . . and it paid him 100-thousand-a-month for two years . . . until he sold it for another bundle. He could do no wrong. He bought the unproductive Matchless, spent thousands developing it . . . and, again, hit a bonanza . . . another one. He developed other mines and hit more riches . . . an unending flow of money. He was the first of the great Bonanza Kings . . .a millionaire many times over. Everything he touched turned to solid-silver . . . at least for a while.

But, there were others who dug in the right places. There was down-and-out John Morrissey who hit it big; he couldn't read or write . . . or even tell time . . . but used some of his new-found wealth to buy a diamond-studded watch. And when someone asked him the time, he'd pull out the watch, show it and say: "See for yourself . . . so you'll know I'm not lying to you." And there was the time Morrissey was asked for just a pittance of his wealth to buy a chandelier for his church, and he agreed . . . even though, he said, nobody around there knew how to play one.

There was Broken Nose Scotty who'd laid out a claim on one of the hills, but preferred the saloons and gambling halls to working. And, one night, he wound up in jail for disturbing the peace. A stranger came in, talked to Broken Nose through the bars, offered him 30-thousand cash for his claim and the offer was quickly accepted. Whereupon, the newly-affluent Mr. Broken

Nose paid the fines of everybody in the jail, bought each one expensive new clothes from head to foot, wined and dined them at the finest restaurant and before midnight, all were broke, and drunk . . . and back in jail for disturbing the peace.

And there were new discoveries, an unbroken string of them, up there on the hills . . . and the silver kept pouring out of the ground. The speculation was frantic, blinding, uncontrolled; properties sold and re-sold within hours and each time, the prices soared. The gambling fever infected everybody . . . even the ladies of the town who set up their own investment club. Men who, a few short months before might have been begging for a hand-out and fighting over 10-cent lunches, now talked casually in thousands and even millions and drank champagne and dined on the finest of foods. Nine out of 10 of the original owners lost out in the feverish wheeling-and-dealing, but others made fortunes without ever setting foot in a mine. There was one mine-owner who sold half-interest in his claim one morning for 50-thousand-dollars; bought it back the next morning, after it had passed through several buyers, for 225-thousand-dollars. Nobody had ever seen anything like it.

Nobody paid much attention when Jim Baxter paid 15-thousand-dollars for a claim up near the top of Fryer Hill. It was just another claim that had sort of been ignored. For months, he worked sinking a shaft . . . but was down more than a hundred-feet and had found nothing. Jim quickly accepted when some tenderfoot strolled by and offered him 30-thousand dollars for the hole. Baxter sealed the deal, called down the shaft to his men to come up; they yelled back they were ready to set off one last shot, but he ordered them to leave it; said he wouldn't put another penny into that worthless hole. And the men left the charge and came on up . . . and helped celebrate the deal.

It was the next morning when the new owners set off the charge . . . and laid open a vein of almost pure silver. Within three months, one side-shaft alone had produced half-a-million; during one 17-hour period, nearly 120-thousand-dollars worth of ore was mined and brought to the surface . . . at a total labor cost of only 60-dollars. The mine was so rich that two of the owners offered their partners 200-thousand-dollars in cash . . . to allow 20 men to work in the mine for only 36-hours . . . and the offer was rejected. Then, one owner offered 10-thousand-dollars to let one man work for just one hour in just one four-foot-square section in one of the tunnels . . . and he was turned down, too. This was the Robert E. Lee . . . the mine that put the cap on the fabulous mines of the district and made Leadville the biggest producer of silver ore the world has ever seen.

But, then came trouble and lots of it. With all that silver and gold pouring out of Carbonate, Iron, Fryer and Breece

Hills . . . and most of it finding its way into only a few pockets . . . there was bound to be trouble . . . and there was. Men had killed each other for a lot less; now they were willing to do the same thing for a lot more.

Claims ran in crazy-quilt patterns over the hills and across the gulches. And there were so many suits and counter-suits that the courts were bogged down . . . but, at least, the lawyers got rich. Armed bands took over many claims . . . simply by threatening the owner or, in some cases of extreme haste, shooting him dead on the spot. Men with money to fight a prolonged court-battle frequently persuaded poorer claim-owners that it was financially healthier somewhere else. Mine owners hired small armies to protect their properties and there were frequent pitched battles in which men on both sides were killed . . . and almost always, these battles wound up in court. Uncle Billy Stevens, who'd helped start this whole thing in the first place, said that of the first 11-million-dollars he took out of his Iron-Silver Mine, he had to spend nine-million in litigation . . . just trying to hang onto it. Uncle Billy said if he had it to do over, he'd forget the legal processes . . . and get a shot-gun and blast any man who set foot on his property.

But it wasn't all killing and fighting and drinking and gambling. Ministers came in early and preached to whomever would listen . . . in taverns, on street-corners, anywhere . . . until churches could be built.

Tabor built his Opera House and held sway from a private box . . . throwing handfuls of silver dollars onto the stage to those performers who captured his unsophisticated fancy. Oscar Wilde came to town and spoke at length here on "The Practical Application of the Aesthetic Theory to Exterior and Interior House Decoration, with Observations on Dress and Personal Ornament". And they sat there, bug-eyed and not understanding a word he said . . . but they liked him. He could, and did, drink with the best of them . . . and that was the measure of any man . . . especially a foreigner who talked big words and wore silk stockings.

Tabor Opera House stage

TABOR
OPERA
MEDICINES
J. S MILLER Co
PHIL

There was the Pioneer Club on State Street . . . the street of nameless girls and fancy ladies such as Josie Mansfield, Winnie Purdy and Lillis Lovell. And the Pioneer Club is still there . . . with bullet-holes in the back bar.

The railroad came in in 1880 . . . the year in which more than nine-million ounces of silver, worth 11-million-dollars, poured down from the hills . . . and there was a lot more where that came from. The newspaper said there were 60-thousand people in the district . . . and Leadville was a grown-up city with brick buildings and fine homes and good hotels and fine restaurants and churches and social clubs . . . and money, lots of money.

In that year of 1880, Horace Tabor had nine-million dollars; he'd been elected Lieutenant Governor; and was spending more and more time in Denver. And he had met a stunning young lady who'd moved over from Central City where the miners had nick-named her Baby Doe. And they were the talk of the town . . . and the state . . . and, only a few years later, of the nation. But, it was 1880 . . . and nothing could go wrong . . . nothing at all.

Elizabeth McCourt Tabor

". . . the miners had nick-named her Baby Doe."

During those 2-years before 1880, the dense pine forests, for miles in all directions, had been frantically chopped down or burned over until, as one writer of the time put it, the hills were as bare as a baby's bottom. Another writer exaggerated, but not much, that "from a lone cabin Leadville became a village in a night, a town in a week, a city in a month and a booming metropolis in a year". In July of '78, there were 15-hundred people in town; six months later, there were 5,000 . . . and at the beginning of 1880, there were 40 to 50-thousand . . . all wanting, and some getting, a piece of the silver pie. And they said it was going to last forever.

By 1880, Leadville was beginning to take on a hint of gentility . . . although not much. It was still wide open and frantic. There were still shootings and stabbings and bombings and fights . . . fights in saloons, in dance halls, on the streets, in the hotels and the theaters . . . wherever one man took a dislike to another man's looks. John Appleby made the mistake of speaking to John Boadman's girlfriend; Boadman simply grabbed Appleby and bit off his nose. Another man, named Davis, got roaring drunk; staggered into a variety hall, jerked the chairs from under some spectators, slugged a few, jumped on a table, blew out the lights, ripped a door off its hinges, shot a goggle-eyed onlooker in the back-side and ran screaming into the night. And, there, they said, was a real man.

". . . and Leadville was a grown-up city with brick buildings . . . good hotels . . . and money, lots of money."

THE PIONEER
GRAND HOT

Nobody knows how many murders were commited in Leadville during those first frenetic years of the silver boom . . . and, actually, nobody cared too much. The cemetery simply wound up with a lot of unnoticed but fresh graves.

But, still they came in that year of 1880. In just one week, during the piercing cold of February, rattling stages, pulled by freezing horses, cursed and whipped by freezing drivers, brought in 700 freezing passengers over those high, snow-packed passes. By summer, when the traveling was a bit easier, more than 150 people were arriving each day . . . many of them from as far away as Europe. During 1880, foreign-born peoples made up more than 25-percent of Leadville's population.

During that year, Horace Tabor had moved an unwilling and complaining Augusta down to a big house in Denver where she kept a milk cow on the lawn . . . and bitterly criticized his extravagances. But, he was Lieutenant Governor with dreams of bigger things, he was the wealthiest man in Colorado; his mines were still pouring out that stream of silver; he owned an interest in the First National Bank of Denver; he had gold mines in the San Juans, silver mines in Aspen, placer mines in Park County, smelters, irrigating canals, toll-roads, copper lands in Texas, grazing lands in southern Colorado, a mahogany forest in Honduras, real estate in Denver, Leadville and Chicago . . . and Baby Doe tucked away in a luxurious suite at the Clarendon.

It was a great year for the bonanza kings of Leadville . . . except for 49-days when the miners got fed up and struck and closed down the mines . . . and the dozen smelters and the four stamp-mills. They were paid a flat one-dollar-85-cents for a 10-hour day, and figured they ought to have more. But, Tabor helped set up the Committee for Safety for Law and Order, got Governor Pitkin to establish martial law . . . and the strike was broken. Anarchists, the miners were called; blood-suckers, the mine-owners were called . . . and the ugly mood hung on far after martial law was lifted . . . after the militia broke camp and went home.

It didn't take long for Leadville to get back to normal . . . such as normal was. There was a certain amount of growing concern over several problems including the shootings. It was suggested that a Sunday closing law be put into effect . . . that all sorts of games, fighting of roosters and dogs, chasing of buttered pigs, and highway robbery he prohibited within the city limits on Sundays. Citizens were to be limited to buying mines, swapping burros, drinking lager beer, singing sacred songs, without getting vicious. But, it didn't work.

In that year of 1880, there were five mostly-wild men to every woman . . . and most of them pretty wild. But, families began moving in and, as in all mining camps eventually, started to bring a bit of grace to the community.

In 1880, one of the newspapers said: "Leadville's society has become cordial, elegant, and radiant with graceful hospitality. Over a year ago, men hesitated to bring their wives and daughters here, but now, all that is changed." Again, that was stretching a point . . . since the fighting and drinking and carousing went on . . . down on State Street and the lower end of Harrison. But, things were, in fact, changing, slowly; maybe for the better, maybe not. One end of town had a look of gentility; there were houses with floors and more than four walls and were even painted; people gossiped about the latest New York and Chicago fashions, the latest books and plays, about politics, liberty and morality, and the price of silver . . . while the other end of town went its merry, raucous, rambunctious way . . . and talked about the price of silver. And all talked and whispered about Horace Tabor . . . and poor Augusta . . . and beautiful Baby Doe, who had moved down into a special suite in the Windsor Hotel in Denver. Tabor was still the richest man in the state; worth millions . . . and an income of 100-thousand-dollars-a-month . . . and still could do no wrong, at least financially. But there were other things to think about and talk about. The Denver and Rio Grande Western came into town that year . . . and there was a celebration. There were rumors that Jesse and Frank James were running a claim in the district, but they weren't; they were running farms and horses in Tennessee. But, it made a good story, for Leadville.

Nobody knew it at the time, but 1880 was Leadville's silver high point. Nearly ten-million-ounces of silver came out of the ground . . . and it was worth nearly 11½-million-dollars . . . and the big mine owners got richer . . . and the miners still worked 10-hours-a-day for $1.85 . . . to $2.00. But, so reckless had been the exploitation of the largest and richest properties, that they were nearing exhaustion . . . even though some of the big ones . . . the Chrysolite, Little Pittsburgh, Matchless, Iron-Silver and others . . . kept production at nine to 10-million-dollars for several years, even with the slow drop in the price of silver.

1883 would be the county's second highest year in production . . . half-a-million in gold, nearly five-million in lead, and 10-million in silver . . . more than 15-million-dollars in that one year. But, then, it was revealed that certain mines had been borrowing heavily to pay dividends . . . and investors panicked and unloaded their shares . . . and broke the market. Stocks dropped from many dollars a share to only a few cents a share. One by one, the Leadville banks went under . . . and Tabor and the other mining kings abandoned Leadville for Denver. The "other end" of town became less noisy as the sporting gentry took off in all directions for greener, if not more golden, or silvery, pastures.

By 1889, there were abandoned shacks all over the district . . . and total production, of everything, was down to nine-million-dollars . . . and people shook their heads almost in disbelief. But none of them was prepared for what happened a few years later . . . in 1893. The mints of India stopped buying silver for coinage; the Sherman Silver Purchase Act was repealed . . . and there it went. The price of silver plummeted . . . and so did Leadville . . . right down a silvery drain. By June of '93, silver was down to 62-cents-an-ounce . . . less than half what

it had been worth; most of the big mines shut down immediately and hundreds of men were thrown out of work. The Herald-Democrat said the Western Union office scored its biggest week, that July, mostly in messages by Leadville store-keepers cancelling shipments of goods they'd ordered . . . and the railroads were loaded with passengers . . . all outgoing. Even the jail, the newspaper said, showed the effects of the depressed times . . . only a half-dozen prisoners to enjoy Jailer Rule's stew . . . the most lonesome place in town, the paper said.

"Those who stayed . . . hitched up their britches, gritted their teeth and hung on . . ."

But, then, to the old-timers who'd known it when, all of Leadville was becoming deserted and lonesome. It was bad, all right, but it wasn't a total disaster . . . since the hills of Lake County still poured out eight-million-dollars in ores that year. The only ones who'd fled were those who'd made their fortunes . . . and the thousands who lived on the ragged edge of survival anyway. Those who stayed, and there were thousands of them, hitched up their britches, gritted their teeth and hung on . . . and looked from those ravaged hills of silver back to that ravaged little gulch where it all had started. Silver might be dying, but California Gulch was still there . . . and . . . it wasn't finished yet.

There were three main topics of discussion, or gossip, in Colorado during that year of 1893 . . . the silver panic, the incredible new gold camp called Cripple Creek . . . and the complete financial destruction of Horace Tabor. It had been more than 10-years since Tabor had gone through two scandals . . . his secret and then public divorce from Augusta, and his secret and then public marriage to Baby Doe. Now, in 1893, the richest man in the state was broke . . . and broken . . .completely. He was to die of a stroke six years later . . . and 44-year-old Baby Doe, would move back to Leadville to live out her days in abysmal poverty.

But, in Leadville, all was not dismal gloom. Men went back to that torn little gulch where it all had started and, amazingly, found it still had more to give. The newspaper said: "The amount of gold is surprising when it's considered that the gulch has been worked almost constantly for 35-years. It has been tunneled and burrowed through in all directions; it has been washed and rewashed; stones and rocks have been moved and re-moved time and again . . . and, each time someone has secured value from the various washings of the pay dirt." And it was . . . incredible that anything at all could have been left . . . . anything at all. Within a few years, gold was found in the Little Jonny mine and for the next 23-years, the district never gave up less than a million-dollars in gold a year. Even so, gold and silver had to take a back seat eventually to the unglamorous, unromantic stuff called zinc . . . 10-million dollars worth of it in 1916 alone. So, Leadville's fabulous life has gone up with gold and down with gold . . . up and down with silver . . . up and down with lead and zinc . . . and then up with a jaw-breaker metal called molybdenum. But that comes later.

In the middle '90's, when Leadville was between booms and feeling a bit sorry for itself, somebody got the idea to take everybody's mind off his troubles . . . and maybe bring in a few tourist dollars . . . by doing something slightly astounding. So, they did something slightly astounding; they built an Ice Palace . . . real, full-scale castle or palace made of huge blocks of ice. And it was, in fact, something . . . complete with 90-foot-high towers, eight-foot-thick-walls, a wooden-truss roof that was supposed to keep it there year after year. In all, this fantastic building was 420-feet long, covered five-acres; had a huge skating rink and a huge dining room and ballrooms and resting rooms complete with maid and valet service. If it were built to take people's minds off their problems, it succeeded. The newspaper raptured: "A burst of splendor and magnificence unmatched and unequalled in the annals of man. The shrunken grasp of greed forgotten for the

Leadville Ice Palace

"And it was, in fact, something . . ."

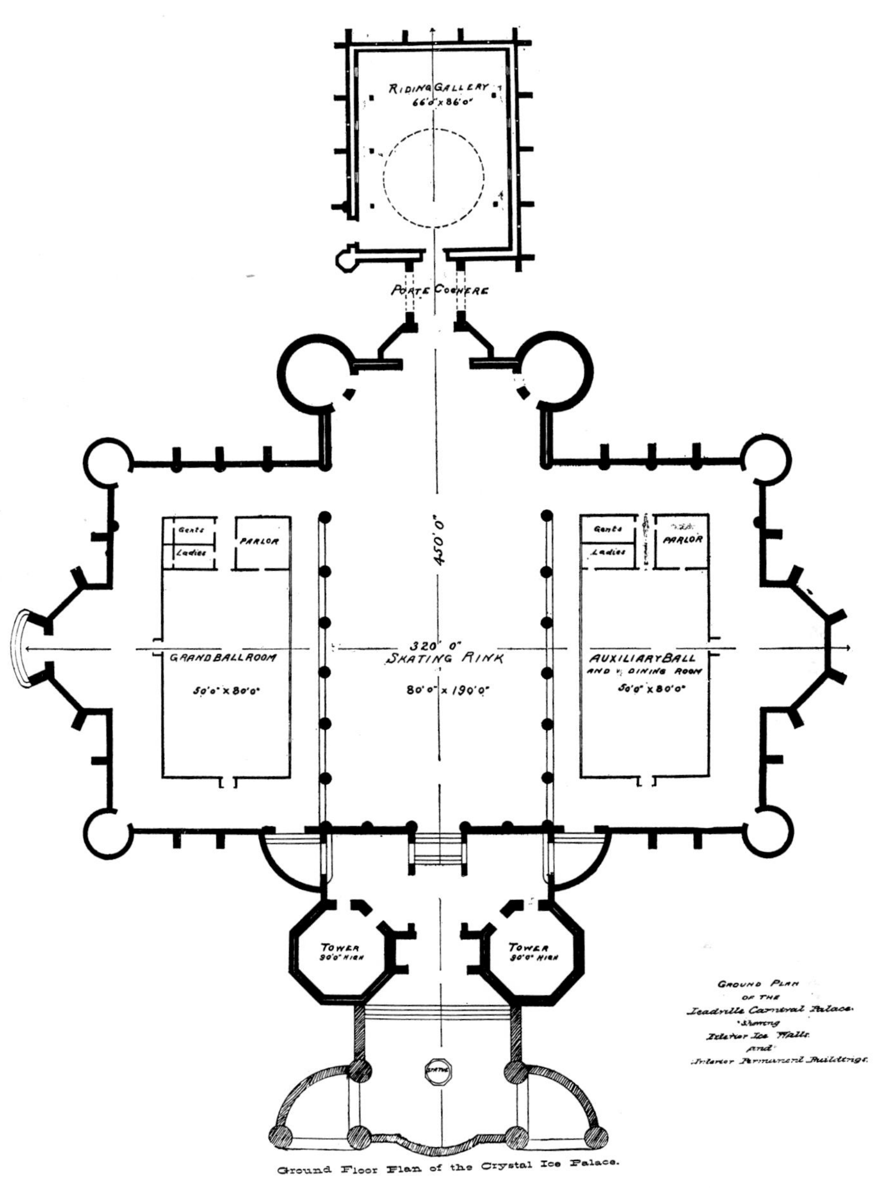

Ground Floor Plan of the Crystal Ice Palace.

time, expands its hands to clasp the joys it would attain; the frozen rivers yielded their crystal covering to please the eye and soften every sign; most glorious vision ever seen by man makes life a glorious dream." And, the Ice Palace was, in fact, that and more. It was a resounding success . . . not for years as planned . . . but only for three-months. And then it melted. Old-timers in the nearly two-mile-high altitude of Leadville had a saying that . . . "Here! there's 10-months of winter and two months of mighty late in the Fall." But, even the old-timers who were used to the bitter cold and stinging blizzards had never seen anything like the storm that began on Wednesday, January 25, 1899. It had been snowing on the surrounding peaks, as usual, and the storm moved down across town. And it didn't stop. By Friday morning, 36-hours later, it was still snowing and there was some glimmer of concern that Leadville might get cut off, but the newspaper tried to calm any fears by saying that the snow will make the sledding better and will fill up the ruts in the streets. And the snow kept falling . . . foot-after-foot. Sixteen-days after the first storm began, the fear was real. On February 9th, the Denver Times said of a new and monstrous storm in Leadville: "The storm continues in all its fury and no trains are moving in or out of the city today. A thousand men will be put to work tomorrow attempting to break the blockade on the rail line; the situation is very serious and is growing worse and if action is not taken soon, hundreds of lives will be lost. All business in the city will be

49

"It was the worst winter anybody could remember . . ."

suspended and attention turned to the shoveling out of the roads. There were only two car-loads of coal left in town, but there were enough provisions for everyone . . . so far." The Colorado Midland, which ran west over Hagerman Pass, was blocked completely, trains were stalled in deep snows or by slides; one long cattle train was caught between slides and every animal slowly froze to death. Huge snow-plows were brought in and hundreds of men shovelled at the rails, but it was useless. The storms in Leadville finally stopped, or at least let up for a while, on March 4th . . . 38 days and umpteen feet of snow after they started, and most of Leadville's immediate problems were over. However, there were more blizzards that winter . . . and the Midland couldn't open its Hagerman Pass route until the weather finally broke in April . . . 78 days after the first bad storm began. It was the worst winter anybody could remember, but nobody suffered much; when the coal ran short; they tore down old buildings for fire-wood . . . and enough supplies managed to get through to keep enough food for everyone. But, they did pray a lot . . . and they shovelled a lot, too.

During those years that followed . . . in the early 1900's . . . the district quieted down considerably from what it had been in those hectic days of the silver discoveries. It continued to turn out anywhere from five to 11-million-dollars a year in gold, silver, copper, lead and lowly zinc.

It was in 1910 that a party was held . . . sort of an unusual party, even for Leadville . . . since it was held 220-feet underground in the Wolftone Mine, and that ladies were invited, despite the old superstitions. It was a rather lavish affair with most everybody in his best bib-and-tucker . . . because it just wasn't every day that you could attend a banquet . . . 200-feet underground.

In the years that led up to the first World War, Leadville got even quieter . . . much to the disgust of the old-timers who still remembered, and preferred, things a bit more wide-open, a bit more noisy, a heck of a lot more interesting. They didn't know it then, but 1916 would be the top year . . . more than 16-million-dollars in valuable minerals came out of the country, out of holes which had been plundered for 40-years and still had more to give. But, then, in 1922 . . . even though the price of silver had bounded back almost to where it was in the old days, production was less than a million for the first time in 56 years . . . and things looked even gloomier. More and more mines closed, or filled up with water; more and more people left the district, or tried to hang on and watch Leadville become mostly a shabby, rickety, weather-beaten ghost of what it was.

Leadville's Victorian past

Part of that ghost was Baby Doe Tabor . . . once the richest woman in the state, young, vibrant and one of the most beautiful. But that was an eternity ago.

Baby Doe, Denver visit 1930's

Three years after Horace Tabor died in 1899, she had gone back to Leadville . . . to the old, worn-out Matchless Mine up there in Little Stray Horse Gulch. He'd told her, just before he died, to hang onto the Matchless, that everything would be all right again. She did . . . but he was wrong. There were some who tried to take it away from her, but there were others . . . many of them not much better off than she was . . . who tried to help as best they could, or whenever she would let them. And she existed . . . alone in her tiny, cluttered shack beside the Matchless, for 35 bitter years. On March 7, 1935, they found her . . . lying, arms outstretched, on the floor of that flimsy cold shack. She had frozen to death. Nobody knew, but it almost looked as though she had planned it that way; that she finally had given full atonement for all her real, and all her imagined, sins.

Matchless Mine shack

54

In the beginning Horace Austin Warner Tabor had been Leadville . . . wild, free-wheeling, wealthy, ambitious, brash and proud. In 1935, Baby Doe was Leadville . . . old, tired, wretched and without hope. After 75-years of being ripped and torn, those old hills of the district had finally given all they had to give . . . more than 500-million-dollars worth of ores . . . and were now empty and exhausted. And it was just a matter of time; everybody knew that . . . and they rubbed their stubbled chins and shook their graying heads at its passing. But, they were wrong again . . . just as they'd been wrong when they thought they'd taken all the gold out of California Gulch, or thought they'd taken most of the rich ore out of Fryer and Breece and Carbonate Hills. It was almost as though those hollowed-out hills had been toying with them all those years . . . first with gold, then silver, then more gold . . . and lead and zinc and copper . . . giving them first one, then the other, by the ton.

There had been some talk, but not much, ever since the silver boom days back in '79 about a strange mineral outcropping up there on Bartlett Mountain . . . just north of Leadville. Just exactly what that stuff was, nobody had any idea. And, anyway, they knew what silver and gold was . . . and there was too much of it around to bother about some unknown something. So, they ignored it; they didn't even bother identifying it for 21-years . . . and then it took another 16-years before anybody decided to mine it. It was something the old-timers could have cared less about, even if they'd known what it was; there was no use for it then. It was a mineral with a jaw-breaker name . . . something called molybdenum . . . hard to spell and even harder to pronounce, and maybe that was one reason they ignored it. But, there was a mountain of the stuff . . . just sitting there, just waiting for all the silver and gold excitement down below to peter out. And when it did, here they came . . . to dig again. They found the metal, simply called moly now, could strengthen steel, increase its heat resistance and wear and rust resistance, they found it needed in electronics and electronical industries . . and in inks and paints and oils and lubricants and even in fertilizers. Bartlett Mountain held back its own unique treasure until it was needed, and, today, it's needed . . . and because of it, the district is humming again. Those old-timers would probably whistle through tobacco-stained teeth if they knew what the mountain gave up in just one year . . . 1969. It produced 90-million-dollars worth of moly and another five-million-dollars worth of tungsten and hundreds-of-thousands-of-dollars of other by-product minerals . . . more in one year than all the gold, silver, lead, zinc and copper taken out of those Leadville hills in the first hectic 25-years. And there's plenty more where that comes from.

". . . those old hills . . . had finally given all they had to give . . ."

There was gold, and lots of it, in the Little Kingdom of Gilpin and in fabulous Cripple Creek; there was silver, and lots of it, in Georgetown and Silverplume and the camps of the San Juans . . . but there never has been a district where so much of everything has been found, and is still being found, as in those should-be-exhausted-but-aren't hills of Lake County . . . up there two-miles high, and still going strong.

There must be lots of ghosts up there on those high, cold peaks . . . up there on once treacherous Mosquito Pass where so many were killed or frozen to death trying to get to the other side. Those grubby, grinning old ghosts must be just sitting up there . . . talking still about the price of silver, and if it goes up any further, some of the old mines will be reopened . . . and everybody knows, they'd say, there's more silver down there than was ever taken out. They're probably moseying around up there . . . still talking among themselves about Horace and Augusta and Baby Doe, or maybe Uncle Billy Stevens or Broken Nose Scotty or Chicken Bill Lovell . . . and certainly about the girls down on old State Street . . . and about the way it used to be . . . way back in those frantic, hard-living, hard-fighting, often-tragic, often-bleak . . . but always good old days. It was something else again, this place . . . and it still is.

Georgetown

". . . but Georgetown was the center of it all . . ."

59

For a long, long time, it was quiet . . . this place where they later built a town. It was quiet . . . simply because it was a hard place to get to, even if there'd been a reason for anybody wanting to get to it. Below, there was a sheer-walled, 20-mile-long canyon; above . . . way above . . . were the knife-sharp and barren ridges of the Continental Divide itself. Even the Utes seemed to ignore this valley; the Spanish are said to have wandered in from the south, but there's no record of it. Trapper and trader Louis Vasquez had a cabin in the valley in the 1830s, but even when elk-hunter George Jackson found gold in a frozen-bar just down the creek away, this part of the valley remained quiet. It's true that some of the searchers from down below rushed this way, squinting and pecking, but there was nothing here, nothing they wanted . . . no sign of what they were looking for . . . and they rushed on. The winds carried faint, disturbing echoes of all the frenzied activity down at Spanish Bar and Chicago Creek and the place they called Idaho; there were even fainter echoes from over the ridge at a place called Central City. But, this part of the valley was ignored . . . until that day, in the summer of 1859, when a lone man fought his way through the dense underbrush and around a big beaver pond . . . and sat down to rest on the hillside. That's when it started.

It was in 1864 that people began to take note of the upper end of the valley . . . and start to build their towns. It had been five-years since George Griffith wearily sat

“In many ways, Georgetown is still the way it was . . . ”

down to rest on that hillside . . . in the exact spot, the only spot in the district, where gold was found. He and his brothers and their father did all right for themselves, but ran into the same problem that was threatening the lives of Idaho and the Gregory Diggings. There was gold and plenty of it, all right, but the ores were refractory and stubborn . . . and, simply, nobody knew how to get it out. It was the same problem with silver. Prospectors found silver in the upper valley when they first came in, but knew of no way of extracting it. And, anyway, silver was scoffed at in those early days since it was worth only 1/16th as much as gold . . . and couldn't be gotten out anyway. But then, five years later, a way was found and the gold camps took on new life . . . and men went looking for silver, too. Three of them . . . Steele, Huff and Layton . . . climbed the forbidding peaks above Georgetown and found it, and named it the Belmont Lode . . . the very first silver mine in the state. Other lodes were opened up . . . the Pelican, the Dives, the Terrible and the Burleigh Tunnel . . . the first mine in the nation to use power drills. And the quiet valley began filling up, bank to bank, with buildings and mills and people and noise. Hair-raising stages roared in daily from Denver over a new route by way of Mount Vernon Canyon and Bergen Park and Floyd Hill and Idaho. And there was whopping and hollering, and a party, the day the narrow-gauge Colorado Central huffed into town in August 1877 . . . as the newspaper put it, eight-thousand people rejoiced. And the silver ore kept tumbling out of the mountainsides and Georgetown kept spreading, and enjoying itself. Other towns sprang up in the gulches and tight valleys higher up, but Georgetown was the center of it all . . . the center for the 25 to 30-thousand people who eventually filled the district.

Georgetown 1867

It became the shopping center and distribution center and transportation center and fun center for the entire district. Whatever anybody had a hankering for, regardless, it was here . . . store-boughten clothing of all sorts, even frills and laces for the ladies; grocery stores, with sawdust on

64

"The people had come to stay . . . and . . . they built their town to last . . ."

the floors, catered to any taste . . . from sow-belly to fresh oysters that had been rushed across the plains in iced-barrels to Denver, then up winding Clear Creek Canyon to the stores and restaurants. There were fresh fruits and vegetables . . . everything . . . all brought in by wagon and freight-car. Everything had to be brought in since the district was too high and too rocky and too un-flat to grow anything. There were meat markets with pork and chicken and fresh beef, very fresh beef, hanging on the walls; take your pick, and pay cash; none of this credit business. You may be loaded today, but broke tomorrow . . . or gone tomorrow . . . to Leadville or Silverton or Central City, or back home to Missouri. Business prospered in the district . . . all from miners who worked 10 to 12-hour days, for up to four whole dollars a day. There was money all over the place . . . inside and outside the mountains . . . and most of it flowed into Georgetown.

On Saturdays, men came down off the hills to kick up their boot-heels. Usually, the barber shop was first stop . . . for a trim and a shave and maybe even a bath in hot water . . . maybe a bath, since one every week or two was enough; a man could catch cold up there if he were too well-scrubbed. All things in moderation, the good book said . . . and they figured that meant soap and water, too.

Georgetown was proud of many things as it grew up . . . its climate, (they said it was so healthful that they had to hang a man to get the cemetery started); it was proud of its schools, its churches, its tree-shaded streets and park, even its law-abidingness. But, it was particularly proud of those fast, fleet-footed, flashy firemen . . . volunteers all. Even if you didn't own a mine or the biggest house in town, you could still be "somebody" . . . as a member of one of the volunteer companies. Membership was limited only to the very best . . . the fastest . . . and the honor and prestige, once a man succeeded in getting in and staying in, was unlimited. But it took some doing to get in and, more especially, to stay in. They had to practice, and practice some more . . . and hard . . . for it wasn't easy and there was a standing line waiting to take each member's place in case he faltered. It was something more than just praise and glory; it was the thrill of being a part of the excitement that surrounded each team; it was also said that young ladies of the town looked with much favor on those muscular young men who raced in the contests . . . especially if they won. The volunteer units included the socially-elite, businessmen, top-rungers and even some low-rungers, but in the company, they were all equal . . . and equally famous. The Georgetown teams took on all comers . . . teams from as far away as Denver and even Pueblo. The day of the big, inter-city contests was a day of celebration . . . the Rose Bowl, the Super Bowl and the World Series all wrapped up

''Georgetown . . . was particularly proud of those fast, fleet-footed, flashy firemen . . .''

CHURCHILL

into one. There was borderline pandemonium as the teams raced the clock, and each other, and often, the Georgetown teams out-raced and out-hosed them all. They won an awful lot of contests . . . and an awful lot of free drinks . . . and, sometimes, in between contests, they even got to race to and fight an honest-to-goodness fire. But, it's too their ever-lasting credit, in good measure, that Georgetown was never hit by a bad fire . . . like Central City or Silver Plume or Cripple Creek or even Creede. To be a member of a volunteer fire-company was just about the best thing that could happen to a man . . . if his legs and his lungs, and his liver, held out. Celebrations were the best days in the mining towns. The

Georgetown hook and ladder company, 1870's

volunteer firemen raced each other; everybody put on his best bib-and-tucker to shoot anvils or go down to take part in, or watch, the big parade . . . especially on the Fourth of July. Every social and fraternal club took part . . . and there were many of them. There were bands, and lots of them, too, which had their own contests . . . and inundated the valley with blasts and clangs and booms that sent the Big Horn skittering up the side of Republican Mountain . . . and brought the miners skittering down. Everybody knew that a town with a volunteer fire department, and a band, and an opera-house or two, and lots of good ore, would be there for a long time to come; it was an indication of permanence and well-being . . . not like some of those camps that flared and died quickly . . . so quicly they didn't have time even for a drum, much less a band. But, Georgetown had all those things and more.

It had the Hotel de Paris, one of the finest and most talked-about hotels anywhere . . . operated by a strange, enigmatic, tight-lipped, irritable Frenchman who called himself Louis Dupuy. He'd been born in France where he learned the culinary arts, had come to America and joined the army and deserted, and changed his name. He wandered to Denver and worked as an itinerant reporter for awhile. He then showed up as a miner in Georgetown until he nearly lost his life in a mine explosion . . . and then started his hotel and nationally-famous dining room. There was nothing like it anywhere, and the food and wine were, they say, unmatched . . . superb food and only the very finest imported wines. It was said that Dupuy carefully chose those who would be allowed to stay in the hotel and sup at his table; that those who, for any reason, incurred his displeasure were instantly sent packing. As a result, it was something of an honor to be allowed to stay in, or dine at, the Hotel de Paris. And the entire region knew of it, and talked about it, and Georgetown took a secret delight in it . . . for 15 years.

To a man earning three to four dollars-a-day, the prices were steep . . . but few objected to paying a whopping 75-cents for a porterhouse steak, or 40-cents for a sirloin . . . since they were perfectly aged and prepared . . . and included bread, butter and potatoes. Or they could order a tenderloin for 60-cents; onions were 10-cents extra . . . or a long list of other foods. The meals were expensive, but the diner had actually eaten at Louis Dupuy's table.

When Dupuy died of pneumonia in October, 1900, after taking his daily bath in icy stream water . . . only then did some of his background come out; he was a mystery man to most to the end. He left his hotel and everything he owned to Aunt Sophie Gally, who was equally mysterious, but who had been his "guest" and employee for many years. Aunt Sophie ran the hotel and restaurant only four months . . . until she,

Louis Dupuy

"There was nothing like it anywhere, and the food and wine were, they say, unmatched . . ."

too, died . . . and was buried beside her longtime friend.

In her will, Aunt Sophie left the hotel to several relatives living in France. Through the years since, the Hotel de Paris has had a succession of owners . . . some of whom came close, but could never equal those 15-years when the strange Frenchman made the name a household word . . . that strange man who called himself Louis Dupuy.

Much of Louis Dupuy's trade came up from Georgetown on the narrow-gauge from Denver . . . people who came up to see and ride on and hold their breaths . . . on the Devil's Gate Viaduct, later called the Georgetown Loop. It was, in fact, an incredible thing . . . this looping, switch-backing, climbing line. From Georgetown to Silver Plume is only 1½ miles, but Silver Plume is a thousand-feet higher. But, despite everything, they decided to put rails up there, and 4½-miles and 3-years later, they had . . . and ore cars came down and tourists went up, in droves . . . at 35-cents-a-head. Of all the absurd places that rails went in the mountains, they said, this was the absurdest. And they were right.

Georgetown continued to grow and to prosper as the silver and lead and zinc and gold continued to pour out of the mountains of the district. The district was turning out around a million-and-a-half in silver and half-a-million in gold each year after full

"Of all the absurd places that rails went in the mountains, they said, this was the absurdest."

production was reached. Even the Silver Panic of 1893 didn't jar Georgetown as much as it did Leadville and the camps of the San Juans, at least, not right away. The price of silver dropped with a thud, but the mines of Georgetown simply turned out more . . . and the district settled back down. But, it was just a matter of time; what had happened to other silver camps would happen to Georgetown, too. Slowly, the cost of labor and the cost of equipment went up . . . and the richest veins started to pinch out. More and more miners and their families found the going progressively more difficult and began to filter away . . . to other towns, to other jobs. The Panic of '93 had broken some of the wealthiest of the towns' wheeler-dealers and, eventually, it broke the district, too. 1896 was the last of the million-dollar silver years in the country . . . and everything was downhill from there on. The price of silver kept dropping . . . from its high of $1.34-an-ounce down to less than a third that amount . . . and production dropped fitfully along with it. One by one, the mines

up above in Silver Plume and the Argentine began to cut back, or shut down entirely. And that seemed to be that. By the end of the First World War, the decline was rapid . . . and George's Town began to look as though it was heading for the same fate as so many old mountain mining towns . . . it looked as though those high barren peaks, and time itself, were slowly but surely squeezing the last flicker of life from the town . . . were trying to take back some of what they had given. And, they did . . . almost.

For a long time, Georgetown was quiet again; the few families who had stayed kept their houses brightly painted and their lawns neat and trimmed . . . and then began to see, and take part in another change. It was after the Second World War that more and more people came driving up the narrow, but paved highway from Denver . . . a transcontinental highway that took pretty much the old stagecoach route up from the plains. Many came to buy and refurbish the old homes . . . to keep them the way they were; to ski in the deep powder of the Divide, or maybe just to look . . . and enjoy. A 70-mile-an-hour, four-lane highway twists up the valley from Floyd Hill past Georgetown through Silver Plume and beyond. It's enough to boggle the minds of those old-timers, if they could see how their valley has changed in such a short time. They used to spend 12 long, wild, swaying, bouncing, kidney-killing hours in a stage from Denver; now, the journey is a comfortable hour or less. They just wouldn't believe it. But, then, we'd be even; it's hard for us to believe some of the things they did, too . . . some of the things they did and thought nothing about.

Georgetown 1870's

If they could walk slowly through the streets of Georgetown today, they'd see much to remind them of the way it was, and some of the things that happened, and some of the people who were there . . . people like Brick Pomeroy and William Hamill and Edward Wolcott and Commodore Stephen Decatur . . . and even Deacon Smith and Billy Barton. Billy ran the famous Barton House in Georgetown . . . one of the best. On June 24th, 1870, he was chosen to lead a delegation down to Denver . . . to help celebrate the arrival of the town's first railroad. The delegation took along a spike of pure silver to be used in the ceremony, but somewhere along the way, Billy and his group stopped off for one or two or several, and ran out of money, and pawned the ceremonial spike. Came time for the big to-do, no Billy Barton, no Georgetown delegation, no silver spike. The Attorney General wrapped an iron spike in white paper and the proceedings proceeded. It was later that Governor John Evans redeemed Georgetown's silver spike from that pawn shop . . . and Billy must have felt terrible, several ways.

And then there was Deacon Smith who used to ride over Union Pass from time to time, from Empire, before Georgetown built its churches. He'd come over to hold services. The Deacon carried a four-foot-long horn to summon the faithful, and after a couple of blasts from that horn, it was hard not to be faithful . . . and not to show up. The Deacon was not to be taken lightly . . . and neither was that horn . . . after what happened to Jericho.

There was the story of the man who came into town one day, and opened up a saloon, and couldn't read or write, and hired a sign-painter who got into an argument with him, and stalked out front to paint: "We sell the worst whiskey, wine and cigars". And the sign brought in so much business, the saloon-keeper . . . even after he was told what the sign said . . . kept it up there . . . until the day he died.

They'd quickly recognize the old Hamill House, if they walked around Georgetown today . . . the house which Joe Watson started in the summer of 1867 . . . a handsome and commodious dwelling, the paper said, which will cost, when completed, not less than 10-thousand-dollars. But, Watson lost the house and his fortune . . . and his brother-in-law, a tough, young millionaire, William Hamill, bought it for only 45-hundred-dollars . . . and spent the next eight years and 50-thousand-dollars on the place . . . until he crashed with silver in 1893 and died, almost penniless, nine years later.

They'd see other houses they'd recognize . . . and maybe remember other things, like that two-day wrestling match up at Brownville . . . and one of the preliminaries that lasted for four-hours-11-minutes, or about Grace Church's new, thousand-dollar, 285-pipe,

25-pedal organ . . . something to hear, they said. They may have remembered reading in the paper about the woman who was found dead of acute alcoholism in her place near Bridal Veil Falls, and the paper saying: "It was the legitimate end of a besotted life; the wave of oblivion has closed over one more wreck of humanity . . . and others are in a sinking condition."

Georgetown had its rowdies, its ruffians, its neer-do-wells . . . but if they caused too much trouble, they were quickly arrested, quickly tried, quickly found guilty, and quickly given a dozen-or-so flicks of a bull-whip, had their heads shaved . . . and told to depart, and they usually did, forthwith. Georgetown was a different mining town; it was different from the beginning. Men who came, many of them, brought their families . . . and came from the East where they'd enjoyed a style of architecture in their homes, and tree-shaded walks and streets, and lawns, and wrought-iron fences . . . and, many of them, a village green. So, they kept as many trees as they could in their town, and planted others in neat rows, and the women had small gardens and lawns in the begrudging soil of the valley. They laid out a park that reminded them of home . . . so many hundreds of lonesome miles away. In the beginning, there were log cabins . . . lined with paper or cotton cloth to keep out the cold. But those gave way to neat, trim, painted houses of sawn lumber, or of brick or stone. The people had come to stay . . . and, for many years, they did; they built their town to last, and for a hundred-years-and-more, it has. And when the old became too old, they built anew. But, carefully.

George Griffith, if he could come walking back up the valley, would recognize it. The hills are the same; the scars have slowly healed over, at least most of them. The impassable beaver ponds and tangled willows have long-since gone in the valley floor, but the hills are the same; they don't change much . . . except for how people change them. George Griffith might be accountably perplexed to find that people don't talk much in Georgetown nowadays about gold and silver . . . the main subject of a hundred years ago; that the town has survived without the mines . . . something the old-timers couldn't even imagine. Without gold and silver, there was no just reason for a town's existence in these mountains. But, Georgetown existed and survived.

Gold and silver aren't talked about much now, but those early-timers and some of the things they did . . . are still. Many of the stories came down the hill from Silver Plume . . . up where most of the big mines were, at the end of a winding shelf-road that took the wind out of many a good horse and donkey. There were silver-bearing veins northeast of Georgetown, and southwest on the Argentine, but the richest veins were found, as they seemingly always were, in the toughest places to get to . . . and from.

And that was up the hill at Silver Plume . . . a little over-nine-thousand-feet above sea-level . . . a comfortable altitude compared with other mines and other towns in the state; didn't take as much breath to operate at this comparatively-low altitude.

Owen Feenan had come up the hill from George's Town to work in one of the early mines in 1868 . . . and, like most miners, went prospecting on his days off. Feenan found something that looked pretty good, but for two-years kept it to himself, told nobody anything about it. But, then, he got sick and it looked as though he were going to die . . . at least, he thought so. So, he whispered his secret to two friends who sadly shook their heads and let him be. Feenan was ill for almost a full year, but recovered . . . and went back up the hill to see what had happened. Much had. His friends had opened the claim, had many men working for them, and a camp had sprung up in the narrow little valley . . . the camp called Silver Plume. It was then Feenan found out that his "friends" didn't even know him; that he'd been cut out entirely. The records don't show Feenan's remarks on the occasion, but it's to be assumed that he felt a degree of animosity. His mine, at least the one he'd found, was the Pelican . . . one of the best producers in the district for a long time to come. It had tapped an eight-foot-thick vein of silver, the richest in the region. But, therein lay trouble. Just a pebble-flick away was the shaft of the Dives Mine and a few brows began to be furrowed. The shafts of the

Pelican and the Dives were so close together, there was a belief that each had dug into the same vein . . . and experts, hired at a hundred-dollars-a-day, agreed. Then the battles started. At one time, there were 23 lawsuits pending . . . and the companies paid hundreds-of-thousands of dollars to mining experts and, more especially, to lawyers. Each mine accused the other of theft; tempers flared. Judge Belford took unusual steps during the many court-hearings; ordered everybody to check his gun at the door, and the Judge kept a brace of pistols on his desk . . . just to make sure things didn't get too far out of hand. The whole county chose up sides in the battling. The two mines kept operating, so close together that the picks of miners in the Pelican could be heard by those in the Dives. When the Pelican got a writ of attachment on all Dives ore, crews of the Dives dug out and shipped 65-thousand-dollars worth of ore on the Sunday before the sheriff could serve the order. Sometime later, miners in the Dives

Silver Plume 1880's

sent to Denver for six coffins . . . to bring out the bodies of six men, they said, who'd been killed underground. The coffins were taken in, then brought back out by grunting and sweating men. Sometime later, the Pelican found that the coffins contained not bodies, but some of the richest high-grade found in the Dives . . , and it was long gone. The battle was finally settled and, later, William Hamill, who managed the Pelican, bought the Dives property for 50-thousand-dollars at a sheriff's sale, and later sold both properties for five-million dollars. Such was the famous battle of the Pelican-Dives . . . one of the most famous in all the high-country.

There were other stories, too, in and on the mountains that squeezed Silver Plume. There was the story of Brick Pomeroy who set out to drive a railroad tunnel through the Continental Divide . . . the great Atlantic and Pacific Tunnel that would carry fast trains from Denver to the Pacific Coast. Brick sold hundreds of shares of stock in his company; boomed that the tunnel would cut endless veins of gold and silver; that it would be a bonanza in the drilling, and when it was finished. It wasn't, either way; no rich veins were cut; no tunnel was finished. They dug a 10-foot-square hole, in fits and spurts, for three-quarters-of-a-mile into the mountain . . . and filled it only with dreams. But, then, it was nothing unique, there were countless thousands of dream-filled shafts and tunnels in these mountains, only a few of which gave anything in return.

They talked of many things, here in Silver Plume and down in Georgetown . . . mostly of gold and silver, but they noted only in passing a brief newspaper note about Mr. Pearce who ran the reduction works down at Swansea in the valley below Georgetown, and a find that he'd made. The paper called it "an interesting discovery" . . . in 1872. Mr. Pearce had found a rather good deposit of a stuff called pitchblende, containing something called uranium. But, then, it was nothing. Uranium, as everybody knew, could be used only for coloring pottery . . . and who needed uranium-colored pottery when a nice tin plate would do just as well.

And so it has gone, this valley . . . this once-hard-to-get-to, and hard-to-get-out-of valley. In many ways, Georgetown is still the way it was . . . similar and yet unique among all the high-country towns. It still operates in the form of a mining district . . . under that special charter granted so many years ago by the territorial legislature. It is the only town in Colorado that has no mayor, because a mayor wasn't called for under that old charter. The police judge and the Board of Selectmen run Georgetown's government, just like in the old days. It worked then; it still works today. George Griffith would like that. This has been only part of the Georgetown story . . . the story that began on that August day so many years ago . . . 100-million-dollars ago. It's a story that may never end. George Griffith would like that, too.

Silverton

"And down in this lush little hole they built their town . . . and called it Silverton."

Baker's Park is a narrow little valley only two-miles wide and three-miles long . . . surrounded by a wall of protective mountains. And down in this lush little hole they built their town . . . and called it Silverton. Some said men who first came into the San Juans got cross-eyed . . . one eye looking for gold, the other eye looking for Utes who didn't take too kindly to these intruders in their beautiful mountains, mountains which had been given to them forever and ever; a government treaty said so. But, the intruders came anyway and pecked at the mountains . . . all the way to their barren tops. And claims were laid out everywhere . . . like the North Star up there about 13-thousand-feet where a man worked five — and rested 10.

And down there in the valley, Francis Snowden built the first cabin in what would be the city limits of Silverton. He was one of the first to come over Stony Pass; his cabin was small and crude . . . and it leaned . . .but it was the gathering place for many of those early arrivals, many dances and parties were held in Snowden's log hut in those early days . . . in the early 70's . . . when things were just getting started.

And the mines grew and the valley towns grew. There was Animas Forks and Eureka and Howardsville and Silverton. And more people came in and the supply wagons got bigger and heavier. And the patient burros kept moseying up and down hair-raising trails with all the nonchalance of a seasoned

mountain goat . . . taking steel rails and everything else up there to the mines. Silverton started getting civilized; wives started coming in and, fussily, began putting things in order . . . their order. They even complained about
cows . . . contentedly meandering the streets. They said it not only was unsightly . . . but also highly unsanitary.

Silverton was doing all right . . . with those heavily-loaded wagons creaking over Stony Pass . . . but it did even better when the little Denver & Rio Grande Western heaved and puffed into town in 1882 . . . 11 years after the town was started. They sometimes, disgustedly, called it the Dangerous & Rapidly Growing Worse . . . but they needed it, and they knew it . . . and it served them well . . . just as it did the big mines and mills, like the Old Hundred tucked away up there in Cunningham Gulch.

The top workings of the Old Hundred were two-thousand-feet from the mill . . . up that sheer cliff. Men couldn't commute, there wasn't that much breath, so dormitories were built at thousand-foot levels . . . and those high structures are still up there, still clinging unbelievably for dear life to a tiny, stratospheric ledge.

Francis Snowden — first resident in Silverton

Stony Pass came down into Cunningham Gulch where the stories and legends are endless . . . like, for instance, the story of the Innis Brothers of New York City who, one day in the early 1870s, decided they ought to have a gold mine. So, naturally, they went to a spiritualist who for a handsome fee, pointed to a spot on a map . . . at the end of Cunningham Gulch. And the Brothers Innis hurried west and staked their claim . . . and, still guided each step of the way by the crystal-ball-gazer, began to dig . . . just as she told them to dig . . . and where she told them to dig. She kept them constantly advised of which direction to run the tunnel . . . suddenly up and then down, to the left and then to the right, zigging and zagging into the mountain. Miners began to get superstitious and began to quit and go to work for other mines in the gulch . . . the Pride of the West, the King William, the Green Mountain, the Leopard and the Osceola. These mines hummed while the Innis Brothers dug and blasted a devious tunnel . . . cutting through rich silver veins, but still driving for that "core of gold" which the spiritualist told them would be there . . . for a fee of fifty-thousand-dollars, she kept telling them. The brothers built a big home up next to their mine . . . at 12-thousand-feet . . . and the money kept pouring into the mountain instead of pouring out of it. Finally, in 1885, they had literally sunk a million-dollars into the mountain . . . in addition to the spiritualist's fee; they sighed deeply and took bankruptcy. Others took over the

Highland Mary, went about it with no help from any crystal-ball . . . and the mine turned out millions in ore, the second biggest producer in the gulch. But the Innis Brothers and their "guiding-hand" will never be forgotten. Just like the prospector who may have been suffering with a morning-after ailment . . . when he found and named his mine "Old Hammer".

Highland Mary Mill — Cunningham Gulch

Old-timers in Silverton still tell, and re-tell, the old stories . . . like the one about Pete Schneider who did quite well for himself in the early days . . . by selling spring water at 50-cents-a-bucket. Pete hauled the water in barrels . . . on wagons in summer and sleds in winter . . . all pulled by dog teams . . . dogs rewarded at the end of each day with an eagerly-awaited shot of red-eye.

And then there was Blair Street . . . the "fun center" of Silverton. Every mining town had such a street and Silverton's was one of the best, or worst, as the case might be. The ladies of the town . . . those who complained about wandering cows . . . also complained mightily about the goings-on along Blair Street . . . about the saloons and the cribs and the opium-dens and about the fun-loving miners who climbed down off the mountains on Saturday and roared into town . . . to roar even louder along Blair Street. But the ladies prevailed.

Silverton 1881

Bat Masterson was called in to do the thing he did best, and he brought some of his tight-lipped, stern-faced cronies with him . . . and they went to work. The jail got a little fuller and the courts were a little busier, but even the famous gun-fighter couldn't put much of a dent in Blair Street. It was like an omen when Mr. Masterson's genteel but ferocious English bulldog was soundly whipped by a Silverton mongrel. But, the town did sorta calm down a bit; it got the cows off the streets anyway.

There has been an argument through the years between Silverton and Cripple Creek. Each claim the "There'll be a Hot Time in the Old Town Tonight" was written there. It applied equally to both camps.

Silverton, like all the high country mining towns, has had its high-highs and low-lows. It began to decline when Congress passed the Sherman Silver Act . . . and all the silver camps panicked. Some hard-rock miners and their families began an exodus, but many stayed to dig for lead and zinc and copper . . . mining, which, on a far smaller scale, is still going on today. As in all old mining towns, there are those who say there is more valuable ore still in those towering, honey-combed, pierced mountains than was ever taken out. That may be, at least in part, wishful thinking. But, Silverton . . . where there may not have been gold but there was silver by the ton . . . keeps hoping. And, who knows . . . it could be right.

94

In 1874, government surveyor Franklin Rhoda marked this valley . . . and its cold, scarred peaks. He wrote: "Not until one has crossed over the several passes leading out of it . . . can he feel a proper regard for this little spot . . . so carefully guarded by nature from the invasion of man". That was 95-years ago. It was true then; it is still true today.

Silverton after 1900

Cinnamon

"Up here, there is no time . . . only the slow changes of seasons."

It took a particular breed of men to work the mines here in the San Juans . . . and in all the other gold and silver camps from Colorado to California. They weren't exactly steeped in the social graces, but they made up for it in other ways; they were sociable and helpful, at least with each other; they were clannish but they fought tooth-and-nail sometimes. They worked hard . . . and they lived hard.

But, when more and more families came in and the ladies began to calm things down a bit, some of that roughness began to be honed off . . . some, not all of it. Sundays were the best time in the mining towns and camps. That was the day of church-going . . . and maybe of a ride up the trails out of town. Or it was a day of getting all the cornet band members together, and taking a picnic lunch in wicker baskets up on the side of the hill where it was cool . . . and where the blast of the horns and the boom of the bass drum was only somewhat terrifying. For the men, who put in 10 to 12 hours-a-day, six-days a week . . . wading in ankle-deep ice-water in the mines, crimping dynamite caps with their teeth, gouging and driving into solid rock . . . for two to 3.50 a-day. Sundays were the best time of all.

One of the towns they lived in was called Howardsville, just around the corner and up the Animas a-ways from Silverton . . . and at the mouth of Cunningham Gulch. It was the county seat when San Juan county was carved out in 1876 and was doing all right until Silverton began to grow . . . simply because it had more room to grow down in Baker's Park. And Howardsville lost out.

There's not much left of Howardsville now . . . except for a lot of stories and legends . . . like the story of John Waters who happily startled everybody when he came down off the snow-clogged pass, in the dead of winter, driving 11 worn-out steers ahead of him . . . and the miners, with a whoop-and-a-holler, poured down off the mountains to bid up the price . . . as

"There's not much left of Howardsville now . . . except for a lot of stories and legends . . ."

quickly as the beef could be slaughtered. It was a great day in Howardsville. Or they tell the story of Moses Hallett, the first federal judge in the district who held court in a small log building. Seems the judge kept seeing the same faces appearing frequently in the jury box and asked the sheriff how come the same men were selected so often, and the sheriff replied, with infinite logic: "The benches are so rough and splintery," he said, "I have to choose only those men who wear leather seats in their britches." And the judge said he'd accept that, that the bench was splintery, too. But, as the road was improved and the rails snaked up the canyon, more and more people left Howardsville and went down to live in the city of Silverton . . . and became some of the first commuters in the state.

Just a few easy miles up the Animas from Howardsville was the town of Eureka . . . a fair-sized and neat town which spread out below the huge Sunnyside mine and mill . . . stair-stepped up the hillside. As many as 500 men worked for the Sunnyside at one time, but like so many other mines and mills, the Sunnyside's life was fitful . . . first up and then down. The up's and down's ended in 1948 when it was torn down for scrap and that was that. In those early days of Eureka, in the 1860s and 70s, many men got out when the first snows came in the fall; they went over Stony Pass or Cinnamon to get away from the numbing cold and snow that lay eight and 10-feet on the level. But, as more comforts came in over the passes, they stayed and weren't too

bad off . . . except when thundering snow or rock slides tore down the mountainsides and ripped out everything. There were stories, many of them, of men being caught and dying . . . and being left where they were 'til the spring thaw. Death in a snow or rock slide was just one way of dying; there were others. And the late-departed might even be missed, at least for a while . . . or he might receive the highest of accolades . . . the tip of a brimming glass at one of the local saloons. He would have done the same for any of them . . . good old "what was his name?"

Up at the end of the gulch, three miles and a couple-of-thousand feet above Eureka, was the locally famous town of Animas Forks . . . the biggest city in the nation, at 11,600 feet. And there was no doubt about it. Probably the most famous story told about Animas Forks was the time a man who'd just been sentenced by a Justice of the Peace announced his intentions of appealing to a higher court, and the Judge said he couldn't because he was standing in the highest court in the United States.

Animas Forks was seemingly plopped down there in 1875 . . . by miners who lived in tents and nearly froze, summer and winter. A year later, there were 30 houses and two big mills . . . including the huge Gold Prince, the biggest concentration mill in the state. Other mills were built, and by 1880, there were 200 people up here . . . sharing what little oxygen there was. That short, bearded little man who'd built roads all over

Sunnyside Mine at Eureka

''It is in the midst of a wild and rugged country where nothing but rich mines would ever induce a human being to live longer than absolutely necessary.''

these mountains, Otto Mears, put in a tool road from Silverton up to Animas Forks, then decided there ought to be a railroad, so he built one. He had carved and blasted out the wagon road up from Eureka; it was his road, and when he decided to run rails on up the gulch, he simply put ties and rails along the old wagon road . . . a grade so steep that a mightily complaining engine could handle only one loaded car going up, and three coming down. But, the story of Animas Forks is not so much its mines and its mills and its railroads, as it is of those tough individuals who stayed and worked there through unbelievable winters. In 1881, the mayor took a look up the hill and warned that what little timber there'd been had been cut down, and there was going to be trouble . . . and there was. That winter, a giant slide started up on Wood Mountain, leaped across the canyon and buried John Haw's cabin in 50-feet of snow; John spent hours digging furiously, and got out. During Christmas week, 1883, when a dozen men, three women and 20 dogs had decided to stick out the winter, it began to snow . . . and left six to 10-feet of snow on the level before it stopped. But, then, right behind it came another of those unbelievable storms that tear at the high country. It lasted for 23 days, and when it ended, they measured 25-feet of snow, on the fairly-level, on main street. One-story buildings were completely covered; men tunnelled from one building to another, or got out on top and snow-shoed into the second floor of the Kalamazoo Hotel . . . the best hotel in the upper part of the county . . . the only hotel in the upper part of the county. But, nobody suffered much; they'd seen past winters and knew what to expect and had laid in more than enough supplies. One of the men said later that one of the first places they'd tunnelled to was the saloon, and from then until the spring thaw, things weren't too rough. But when spring came, they were knee-deep in mud . . . and it was then they heard that around 20 men had been killed by slides at the mines up in the basins where they'd been spending the winter. Living in the mountain shanty towns was never easy, but Animas Forks bested the worst of them. And it, literally, went downhill rapidly. One visitor from the East took one look and wrote: "It is in the midst of a wild and rugged country where nothing but rich mines would ever induce a human being to live longer than absolutely necessary." The visitor had a point.

"It's a difficult place to get to; it's even more difficult to leave."

There wasn't a mountain or a valley of the San Juans that wasn't pecked over during those first years of the rush, but it was almost 10-years later that a man by the name of Christopher J. Carson . . . not the famous Kit Carson . . . found mineral all over the place, right on top of the Continental Divide, up there above 12-thousand lung-hurting feet. There were other places where the ore veins were killers to work; there were higher mines over around Silverton, but Old Carson had unique problems of its own . . . just because it was where it was . . . right up there on the very chilling, giddy top of the world. However, Carson could and did boast that it did not have one problem that most of the other camps had; it was not threatened by snow-slides . . . since it, literally, was above all that . . . and most everything else, too. However, Carson was built on a solid dike of iron, and lightning storms were and are hair-raising. But, despite the fantastic storms, shrieking winds and numbing cold, more than a hundred men worked the mines up there summer and winter . . . and took out hundreds-of-thousands of dollars worth of silver. The mines up there on top had been working for 15-years when somebody stumbled across gold just two miles away . . . on the north slope of the Divide . . . down below timber-line. And the town was also named Carson . . . Old Carson up on top; New Carson down here. All high-country miners were a special breed of men, but those who worked and lived in the two Carsons had to be an extra-special breed. Burrows Park and some of the other camps thought they had supply problems, but the two Carsons faced infinitely more . . . perched where they were. For 15-years, the only supply route was little more than a trail that snaked up Lost Trail Creek from the Stony Pass road. It was years before a wagon road was shoved up Wager Gulch from the Cinnamon Pass road on the north, but once they had their road, they kept it open, almost unbelievably, winter and summer. When the spring runoff took out the road, they put down their miner's picks, took their shovels and went down and fixed it; when heavy snow blocked the road in winter, they laid down their miner's picks, took their shovels and went down and opened it. They were incredible men . . . but no lesser men could have done what they set out to do, and survive. Men stayed up there and continued to work right on through the Silver Panic of 1893 when hundreds of mines were forced to close and men went in all directions . . . away from the district . . . to look for something else. They stayed up there and continued to work even though they heard fabulous stories of the fabulous new gold strike up behind Pikes Peak . . . a place called Cripple Creek. Finally, in the early 1900s, they came down from their high towns and left them to the winds that still shriek, snows that still swirl, and the lightning that still plays fretfully around the peaks . . . but with nobody, now, to hear or see.

Up here, there is no time . . . only the slow changes of seasons. Maybe that's why they stayed, despite the hardships, longer than they should. It's a difficult place to get to; it's even more difficult to leave.

Near the eastern end of the Cinnamon Pass Road is San Cristobal . . . the lake known to the Indians for hundreds of generations and later to trappers and prospectors and mine-owners and town-builders. It was the junction of the Cinnamon route and the Los Pinos route. It was the Los Pinos Road which sped toward the silverboom area of the San Juans and was built by that one-hundred-pound string of firecrackers that kept exploding in all directions, Otto Mears. He and Enos Hotchkiss took dead aim on Lake San Cristobal and the silver mines beyond and shoved their road through . . . despite a few impolite objections from the Utes who had believed for several hundred years that this was their land. But, nobody took them seriously. And, as it had done in so many other places at so many other times, gold and silver won out. Nobody ever doubted that it wouldn't, except maybe for some of those young Ute braves who didn't believe all those solemn promises. Enos Hotchkiss was doing fine on his road until he spotted float on the hillside at the lower end of San Cristobal and started to dig for gold and found it . . . and road-building suddenly became less attractive for a while. The Indians were right when they said the lake had been there far longer than anybody could remember. Experts who came later and who knew about

such things said San Cristobal must have been formed 700-years-ago when the entire side of a mountain gave way and boomed rock and mud and debris 26-hundred-feet down the four-mile-long gully . . . and dammed the stream. The ripping and tearing must have been heard for miles in all directions, if there was anybody around to hear it. Reckless pine and aspen have taken root on the slide, which is still sliding at 15 to 20-feet-a-year, down that gulch. And that makes the trees the fastest moving stand of timber anywhere in the state. It was this slide which the old-timers called Slumgullion . . . because, they said, it was sorta mixed-up . . . and looked like a stew, especially the stews they made out of anything and everything available over their campfires.

Down near the bottom and to the side of the Slumgullion Slide there's a marker in memory of five men who gave so much of themselves to their erstwhile guide, a 190-pound, black-bearded, quick-tempered, hatchet-armed man . . . named Alfred Packer. The story of Packer has been told and re-told . . . several different versions by Packer himself, but nobody will ever know exactly what happened that day near Lake San Cristobal when Packer set-to with his hatchet on his five companions . . . there in the deep snow on Cannibal Plateau. Packer went to prison for 40-years, but was paroled after only four . . . and lived out his life, they said, being nice to little children and stray cats . . . and as a strict vegetarian.

And down there below Cannibal Plateau, where the valley widens a bit and flattens a bit is Lake City . . . the eastern end of Cinnamon Pass. When Otto Mears and Enos Hotchkiss came down off Slumgullion with their new road from the east, there were a few tents here . . . nothing more. Some of the mines had been started, like the Ute-Ulay up Henson Creek, but nothing much could be done until the snows melted in the spring of 1874. Then Mears, exploding again, helped found Lake City that fall, and started the first newspaper there in '75 to tell the world about the new town that his Saguache store was supplying, with his wagons, of course. But Mears didn't have to sell the San Juans to anybody; hundreds already were hob-nailing all over themselves and each other to get there. In two years, Lake City jumped to a thousand population . . . a thousand people who hadn't rushed on up the gullies and over the ridges, had stopped here. There was enough of everything for everybody . . . couple of banks, two pool halls, seven saloons, four hotels, four Chinese laundries, two breweries and a couple of cigar factories . . . and 15 lawyers. And, as mining towns went, Lake City was pretty quiet most of the time . . . since policemen got a flat-five-dollars for every

Lake City

WOMENS CLUB
CAFE
GIFTS
LEAT

man they arrested and convicted of whatever. And the list of "whatevers" that would get a man arrested and convicted was a long one.

Churches came early to Lake City, unlike some of the other camps. Brothers Alexander and George Darley arrived on June 17, 1876, organized the Presbyterian church, held services the very next day . . . attended by 115 people and, by November, had their church built . . . the first on the Western slope. There were five other churches in town and the ministers walked or snowshoed to outlying camps to hold services. It was said that the ministers, especially the Darley brothers, commanded the respect even of gamblers and saloon-keepers; that gambling games actually adjourned to hear them preach. So, Lake City was uncommonly well-behaved . . . because of the churches, and that five-dollar-a-crime fee to the police.

Lake City is fairly quiet still . . . except maybe on a summer tourist evening — or until a plane wanders over, buzzes town, and somebody shoos the kids and dogs off River Street so it can land. Lake City is not quite what it was a little over 90-years ago . . . but neither is Silverton . . . or that high road in-between. But time is using a slow, soft eraser on the rest . . . on those scars up there on the hillside and on the dumps and the old camps . . . on all except the faint echoes that drift aimlessly down the canyons, lonesome . . . but not completely forgotten.

Cripple Creek

"What ever it was, it was here . . . and it's still here . . . in this incredible place called Cripple Creek."

"Not one century, nor five centuries will see the Cripple Creek mines exhausted. The grandchildren of our children's children will not see the end of gold-mining in the hills that belt the Cripple Creek District. A century from now will see Cripple Creek the metropolis of a great mining district . . . extending 25-miles North and South, and 10-miles East and West . . . with blocks of magnificent brick and stone fronts lining its thoroughfares, and with palatial and royally-furnished residences dotting its suburbs . . . with its lofty church-spires lifting into the blue ether of our mountains . . . with its 500-mills grinding and pounding away upon the daily product of the mines, and finally, with its quarter-of-a-million energetic, progressive, law-abiding people."

"It took not one century or five centuries . . . it took less than 70-years . . . so frantic was the ripping, tearing, gouging of the Cripple Creek hills . . . the unbridled gutting of this small but immensely rich pocket of gold."

The earth here would be generous, but for a long time it held its secret . . . and was quiet and untroubled. Its high meadows on the sloping, undulating west shoulder of Pike's Peak were green; its rounded hills were blanketed with black-green pine and fluttering aspen groves that spilled down into peaceful hollows. It was remote and serene and beautiful and . . . unscarred.

Men had crossed and re-crossed this high, rolling area . . . Spanish explorers, French and American trappers, surveyors . . . then the floods of silver and gold-seekers that went around or through these hills . . . the floods that poured to some distant strike, then back again. Few paused here; it was the least likely-looking of all . . . for what they were seeking.

Bob Womack

Then, other men came into the district . . . looking for something else . . . a place to live. They brought their cattle to the rich, green slopes . . . and they built cabins and worked hard and lived quietly. Despite the 10-thousand-foot height, the winters weren't too severe and the summers cool and pleasant. One of those who came to this place was a cow-boy . . . Bob Womack. He built a small, log cabin near the mouth of the hollow he called Poverty Gulch . . . and he was content, at least at first.

That was in 1876 . . . 16-years after most of the gold discoveries in the state, and the year Colorado whooped and hollered when it became a state . . . and everybody was talking about the fantastic silver ore pouring out of the ground over at Leadville. Like everybody else, Womack talked about it and dreamed about it . . . and, as he rode the hills of Cripple Creek, he looked for tell-tale signs of ore, and he found it . . . and he told them down in the Springs again and again there was gold up there . . . and they'd smile knowing smiles and go their way. Some listened, and came and dug, and went away again.

It was almost 13-years later . . . in 1890 . . . that Womack staked his first claim, in Poverty Gulch, and named it the El Paso lode . . . and in the Springs, they continued to smile . . . most of them anyway. Hadn't there been the Pisgah hoax; somebody should have been hanged for that one.

But, in the spring of 1891, a part-time carpenter, part-time prospector came up to see what Bob was talking about; came up from Colorado Springs where he was known as a rather peculiar man . . . a strange man who worked as a carpenter until he got himself a grubstake, then took off into the hills on his never-ending search . . . a search that had been going on, for him, for nearly 20-years. His name was Winfield Scott Stratton. He looked over the hills and told Womack it was the least-promising spot he'd ever seen, but he staked four claims, gave them away and went home. Stratton came back in the summer and staked out several more claims . . . at the south end of the district because, he said, he wanted to get away from the tenderfeet up at the north end who were blowing themselves to smithereens with dynamite. One of those Stratton laid out, on the southeast slope of Battle Mountain, was one he called The Independence. It was the fourth of July. And he began trying to sell his claims for $500 each, and there were no takers . . . at least not for the Independence. It was just as well; Stratton later sold it for 10-million-dollars and the mine eventually produced a total of 28-million in gold . . . and gold was less

Winfield Scott Stratton

than $21 an ounce. Until he died 11-years later, Stratton was the "heart" of the district . . . that peculiar man who gave of his time, his money, and so much of himself to any and all who needed it . . . even to the penniless Silver King, H. A. W. Tabor.

Stratton, more than any other man or group of men, was Cripple Creek.

Two red-faced and dog-tired Irishmen had followed Stratton up from the Springs. They were the tenderest of tender-feet; 41-year-old plumber Jimmy Burns and 23-year-old errand boy Jimmy Doyle. But, they'd gotten there too late; everything was already taken . . . .well, almost everything. They found a long, narrow, ribbon-like piece of ground above Stratton's Independence, so they took it . . . and started to dig. And they dug and dug and cussed and argued. When they were down 30-feet and still had found nothing . . . since they didn't know what they were supposed to be looking for . . .Stratton's cook, John Harnan, ambled by and was told, pleadingly, that if he'd please show the ex-plumber and ex-errand boy what they were supposed to be digging for, they'd give him a third. He did; about half way down the hole, Harnan found they'd cut right through one of the richest veins anywhere. Burns and Doyle, those wild-eyed Irishmen, named their mine The Portland. Eventually, the property would produce more than 61-million-dollars.

And then there was Sam Strong, a hard-living roustabout, who decided he ought to have a claim of his own. He staked one, sold it for 60-thousand-dollars, then went on to become one of the district's millionaires . . . before he caught a shot-gun blast in the middle at the Newport Saloon up in Cripple Creek. Sam didn't live to see his Strong mine, the one he sold for 60-thousand, eventually produce more than 13-million.

Frank and Harry Woods came into the district and took a thousand-dollar gamble. They bought the old Mt. Rosa placer claim down below Battle Mountain, and laid out a town-site . . . and set out to get rich selling lots. They got rich, all right. They were blasting for the basement of their new hotel . . . in the town they'd named Victor . . . and knocked a hole in a 20-inch vein . . . and started withdrawing 50-thousand-a-month. They named their mine the Gold Coin and built the largest and flashiest shaft-house in the district . . . even to stained-glass windows. But, then, it wasn't every man-jack who came along and made that kind of money . . . out of digging a basement.

Over on the other side of Battle Mountain, near the head of a dry gulch, was a hole-in-the-ground . . . just a hole-in-the-ground . . . called the Cresson. Its owners watched tons of ore pour from surrounding mines, and kept digging. But, that's all they did . . . dig and pour more money into the hole. And they dug and poured in money for 20-long and disappointing years. But, in 1914, when some of the others had given up the ghost, the Cresson was down 12-hundred-feet . . . and in one of the cross-cuts, they found it . . . a roomful of gold. Miners call it a "vug" . . . sort of a cave lined with sparkling crystals of gold. When they found it, miners used garden hoes to scrape it off the walls, then stoped the area around the cave . . . and took out nearly one-and-a-quarter-million-dollars. And the owners declared a dividend. The old Cresson, the object of many a wry smile for

20-years, hung on until 1961 . . . and when it closed had given up 51-million-dollars. There were others in the district . . . big ones and little ones . . . each with its own stories, some true, some enlarged in the retelling . . . and by time itself. There was the Vindicator which produced 28-million; the Ajax, 30-million; the Elkton, 16-million; the Empire Lee, 15-million. There was the Last Dollar which produced 7½-million, and

Cresson Mine

the Cycle which poured out 23-million; the El Paso, 10-million and the Dr. Jack Pot, 7-million. There were others, many of them . . . and the world had never seen anything like it. From the very beginning, Cripple Creek caught the imagination of the nation; it was a head-shaker; it was a life-saver. As gold camps go, Cripple was late in coming . . . and luckily . . . for the state and the nation, and more especially for the thousands of men who'd been in these Rocky Mountains for 20-years grubbing out a dangerous living, but, at least, it was a living. It was in 1893, two years after Cripple blossomed, that the government repealed the Sherman Silver Act . . . and the price of silver, then the back-bone of Colorado's economy, plummeted. Most of the state's mines closed and thousands of miners were without even their normal dangerous living. And the nationwide depression grew worse. But, there was Cripple Creek . . . high, bright, incredibly rich . . . and ready. Desitute miners and their families, destitute businessmen and temporarily-destitute gamblers . . . destitute everybody from the silver towns poured into the new camp. And the union was good. Cripple Creek gave them what they needed . . . and they, in turn, gave the district what it needed . . . and both prospered. But, then, some prospered more than others . . . and there was trouble.

"No place can be all things to all men, but Cripple Creek came close."

At the end of Cripple Creek's first year, only three mines had shipped any ore . . . only 200-thousand-dollars worth. By 1894, three years later, there were 175 producing mines that produced 2½-million . . . and only the surface had been gouged. And everybody knew it . . . especially the fledgling Western Federation of Miners who came in to see what could be done. Some men were working eight-hours for $3.00, but others were being paid only $3.00 for nine-hours. There was grumbling that got louder and finally came to a head when the big Pharmacist Mine up on Bull Hill cut the pay for eight-hours work to only $2.50. The miners struck . . . for $3.00 for eight-hours. The mine-owners refused; trouble began; the state militia was called out . . . and the argument was finally settled . . . and the union won its argument. But, nine-years later came the bloodiest strike . . . one that lasted 130-days. Both sides were armed camps, and men were killed on both sides, and

Cripple Creek Strike, 1903

again the militia was called in . . . and Harry Orchard, one of many hired thugs, blew up the Independence train station and killed or injured 25 non-union men. The clamps went on and scores of union miners were escorted to the Kansas and New Mexico borders and told never to come back. And that was that . . . and the mines reopened.

Strike 1903. Prisoners being escorted to courthouse from the depot by military

The Cripple Creek ore-producing area was small . . . only four-miles wide and six-miles long. But, snuggled in or perched on and around the rolling hills of that compact area were no less than a dozen towns. There was Gillette on the north and Victor on the south, and in between were Goldfield and Independence, Anaconda and Elkton, Cameron and Altman . . . the highest incorporated town in the nation. And there was Lawrence and Arequa, Midway and Cripple Creek Town itself. There were others, but they died out or were absorbed. Some old-timers, still living in Cripple Creek, say there were more than 80-thousand people squeezed into this tiny area at its peak, but it's doubtful there ever were more than 50-thousand at any one time . . . even including all the curious from Denver and the Springs who came up to see what was going on. But, still, 50-thousand is a lot of people to be crammed into such a small area.

In the spring of 1896, Cripple Creek Town covered 600-acres and was still growing . . . a spreading, ugly jumble of hastily-built and dust-dry fire-traps. There were only a few solid buildings in town, and the whole place was over-ripe for trouble. It came on a Saturday morning in April . . . a bright, sunny, windy day. A local bartender slapped his girl-friend at the Central Dance Hall; she came at him with a knife; he grabbed her arm, and they upset a lighted oil stove. And it started . . . and ran crackling and spreading before the brisk south wind. In desperation, firemen dynamited a 200-foot stretch of shacks on 3rd Avenue, but the flames went around. Dozens of flimsy buildings flared and left nothing but ashes . . . and 15-hundred people were homeless. The fire had lasted only three-hours, but the town took care of its own and began a quick recovery.

Four days later, much of the debris had already been carted away and crews had started to rebuild the destroyed saloons and parlor houses and business-houses and homes. And the wind came up from the south again, and in the old ramshackle Portland hotel, a careless maid tipped over a

Cripple Creek fire 1896

''And it started . . . and ran crackling and spreading before the brisk south wind.''

pan of hot grease on the stove . . . and flames jumped. Just an hour later, the roof of the hotel caved in and sent billows of embers into the air. The Palace Hotel caught fire and its boilers exploded with a deafening roar, and 700-pounds of dynamite went off in a grocery store, and every building along Bennett Avenue west of 3rd caught fire. The heat was so intense that gold and silver in Dave Moffat's Bi-Metallic bank melted and ran out of the drawers. By nightfall, it was all over . . . and five thousand people had nothing, and much of Cripple Creek, because of two fires in four-days, was a cinder heap. Down in the

After the fire

Bennett Avenue

Springs, Stratton heard of the trouble; he quickly collected emergency food and tents and supplies enough for two-thousand-people . . . and two Midland locomotives took out up the 4-percent Ute Pass Grade at 15-miles-an-hour. And, the next day, another train of supplies came up the mountain. Within 48-hours, all five-thousand homeless had been sheltered and were eating, as Marshall Sprague put it, a small breakfast of hot cakes, biscuits, pork chops and coffee . . . and two big meals a day. The fires, some said, were tragic, but were blessings in disguise. Now, they said, Cripple Creek could build orderly, and of brick and stone, and it did. And many of those old and solid structures are still there today . . . still lined up wall-to-wall along Bennett Avenue . . . the only street in the world, they say, where you can fall off the middle of a street and break your neck. And, it's possible.

After the 1896 fires, Cripple Creek's population jumped again . . . up to 40-thousand . . . and the mines grew in number and kept pouring out an ever-increasing golden stream of money. By 1903, there were 475 mines which produced a whopping 18-million-dollars . . . the biggest year the district ever was to have. There was a slow decline in production after 1903, but nobody paid much attention; there were still millions coming out of the deepening holes each year, and the deeper the mines went, the richer the ore became. But, deeper holes meant higher costs . . . and big business began to move in from the outside and consolidate various properties. In addition to higher costs, there was another problem . . . one that, many years later, finally helped bring the district to its knees. The problem, simply, was water. The thick granite sides of the bowl that held the gold also held water, and as the mines went deeper, bigger and bigger pumps were needed to keep the holes dry . . . or try to anyway . . . and costs soared. Until someone proposed to go down the mountain, drive a tunnel that would pierce that granite bowl and drain the mines. And they did, and it worked. Six-years later, deeper mines and more water and another tunnel . . . a longer and deeper one . . . the Roosevelt which did its job and lowered the water-level in the bowl 700-vertical feet. But, then, in 1939, the same trouble again . . . so crews went far down the canyon southwest of Victor and drilled a six-mile-long tunnel into that bowl . . . and intersected the shaft of the big Portland Mine 32-hundred-feet below the surface. And drained all the interconnected mines in only two days. This is the Carleton Tunnel . . . finished in 1941 and named for one of those incredible men of the district, A. E. Carleton . . . a young college graduate with only one-lung who came west to die in 1880; and did . . . in 1931 after becoming immensely wealthy on ingenuity, hard-work and Cripple Creek gold. Water still flows, still pours from the Carleton . . . from 32-hundred-feet in the old Portlands and the Ajax . . . and before the Ajax up there was shut down, miners had sunk a winze 52-feet past that 32-hundred-foot level . . . and

pumps had to be used to keep out the water. It was just like the old days.

The Cripple Creek District was different from other camps in many ways. One was that it was the only mining area in the world where men could ride to and from work on electric trolley-cars. There were two electric lines . . . the High Line and the Low Line which snaked in around and through the various towns and the growing mine dumps. The lines kept running until 1919 . . . until fire destroyed the car-barns and much of the equipment. But, by then, the district had dwindled to less than six-thousand people and only 41 mines continued to operate. Even so, the 41 produced 5½-million in gold that year . . . and that was when gold was still worth less than $21-an-ounce.

And there were the railroads . . . three of them . . . and all the result of considerable cost and intestinal fortitude. The first to snake into the district came up Phantom Canyon into Victor from the South. It was the narrow-gauge Florence and Cripple Creek which got an 18-month head-start on the Midland which pushed its standard-gauge rails in from the North. It was just as well the F&CC had the head-start; it paid all of its construction costs in that year-and-a-half, but after the Midland came in, the little narrow-gauge never made another dime.

And then there was the Colorado Springs and Cripple Creek District Railroad . . . the Short Line . . . which climbed up behind

Florence and Cripple Creek Railroad

423. PHANTOM CAÑON
ON THE
PHOTO BY McCLURE
DENVER

Cheyenne Mountain and dynamited a route around the south side of Pike's Peak. Teddy Roosevelt, that gad-fly public servant who was everywhere, rode the Short Line and said the scenery bankrupted the English language. And it did . . . and it still does . . . and, except for the rails and ties, the road-bed is still there and easily driveable. It's now called the Gold Camp Road.

The Midland Terminal came south from the main-line at Divide . . . after that exhausting climb from Colorado City through the Ute Pass, the looping switch-back at Woodland Park, then westward. It was some railroad, but then there wasn't any railroad in the high country . . . and there were miles of them . . . that wasn't something. Rails had no business being in this country, but then, Cripple Creek had no business being where it was, either.

Cripple Creek still hums, but it's a muted hum nowadays . . . and only in the summer when people come from everywhere to this place which saw so much and did so much and gave so much in its brief, hectic, romantic, tragic, funny, incredible life. They come because the district still has much to tell and show and be proud of.

There's the old Midland Terminal depot standing solidly at the east end of Bennett Avenue . . . now a museum, a storehouse filled with the bits and pieces of yesterday. And a few ghosts.

Colorado Springs and Cripple Creek Railroad

Myers Avenue is still there . . . and so is Hazel Vernon's "Homestead" but the others . . . the many others . . . are gone, and the street is dusty and quiet.

There is a road now to the top of Mt. Pisgah . . . that old volcanic cone which has looked down on so very much . . . up past the cemetery where so much of the district's history is buried.

There's the old Molly Kathleen on the hill above Cripple Creek town . . . once a working mine, but now a mecca for vistors who can see for themselves where and how men blasted and dug through solid rock following those elusive veins so many years ago.

And, in Victor and in Cripple Creek, there are still homes . . . some new but most old . . . old homes which have been refurbished and given new faces by those who refuse to let the district die. There are old-timers who still talk of gold and the way things were . . . once; there are others who still peck at the ground . . . and talk of gold; there are new-comers who talk of the way things were, and are, and may be again . . . someday.

And there's the Imperial . . . the old-new hotel . . . which has helped Cripple Creek survive . . . the center of today in this yesterday-setting.

No place can be all things to all men, but Cripple Creek came close. This tiny, ravaged spot gave its millions in gold, and lasting fortunes, to errand boys and plumbers, to grimy prospectors and coal-merchants, to lumbermen and roustabouts, to druggists and butchers and grocers and even a school-teacher . . . millionaires all. It gave renewed life and hope to thousands of nameless men who crimped dynamite-caps with their teeth, and drilled and stoped and mucked deep in the earth for $3.00-a-day and fought for that; its 500-million-dollars in ore put a solid gold prop under the state and the nation itself. Cripple Creek was the fountain-head of stories that became legends that have been told and re-told . . . some true, some not. They were the legends of Womack and Stratton, of Soapy Smith and Joe Wolfe and Kid Meadows, of Jack Dempsey and Texas Guinan. There were the legendary Bert Carleton, Big Bill Heywood and Dick Roelofs . . . and Hazel Vernon and Pearl LaVere and Lola Livingston, and even that smart-aleck dude from the East, Julian Street. They were all here . . . drab and flambouyant, wealthy and poor, suckers and takers, and honest and otherwise. And their stories are endless.

If you sit quietly up on Bull Hill or Battle Mountain . . . or at Altman or down in the hollow at decaying Independence . . . you might even hear it . . . the squeal of flanges on iron rails; the quiver of the earth from rumbling explosions deep beneath you; the rattle of ore-carts and wagons, the shouts and curses and even maybe . . . the tinkle of a piano in one of the old saloons. Whatever it was, it was here . . . and it's still here . . . in this incredible place called Cripple Creek.

Creede

"The old timers used to say . . . there were only two months of the year . . . Winter and the Fourth of July."

It's not a very big place . . . this place called Creede. It never was very big and didn't last very long . . . but while it did, everybody knew about it, and talked about it, and even shook their heads at some of the things it did . . . since there was little if anything to be done that Creede didn't do.

The old-timers used to say of this section of the state . . . there were only two months of the year . . . Winter and the Fourth of July. They may have been stretching the truth a little bit, as they often were inclined to do, but in the 1870's . . . when the only way to move around in this high country was by foot . . . it may, indeed, have seemed as though summer came and went all too quickly. And the long winters then were, in fact, hard and seemingly endless. And if men moved around . . . if they moved at all in the hard months . . . it was only with great effort . . . and with a very good reason. The winters in Creede, and in all the towns of the high country, are still hard . . . but not like they were, once. But then, Creede isn't like it was, once, either . . . and yet it's one of the youngest of all the bonanza towns, the boom towns. By the time it started, in 1891, Silverton, and Ouray and Lake City . . . over on the other side of those impossible mountains . . . had been going strong for more than 15-years; millions in silver were still pouring out of the ground up at Leadville and Baby Doe had just given birth to her second daughter up in Denver and everybody was talking about the name her parents gave her . . . Rosemary Silver Dollar

Echo Honeymoon Tabor . . . born with a solid silver spoon in her mouth . . . and peacocks on the lawn. By the time Creede came along, there were nearly half-a-million people in the 14-year-old state, with railroads running the length and breadth of it, new roads all over the place, colleges in Fort Collins and Greeley and Denver and Colorado Springs; already famous opera houses in Denver and Central City and Leadville, humming steel mills in Pueblo . . . and Nathan Meeker had been dead for 11-years. By the time Creede came along, the Utes had been out of the area for nearly twenty-years and it had been two-years since the last flick of Ute anger . . . when Colorow led a small band into Colorado from their bleak reservation in Utah and was driven back . . . for good. By the time Creede came along, the state was getting plumb civilized and almost dull . . . almost, but not quite. There were still enough of the old-timers around, and enough action in the mountain towns, to satisfy them. The gambling halls and the saloons were still wild enough to suit everybody . . . except maybe wives. There were still enough bare-knuckle fights and gunnings to keep Canon City well attended, and keep selling newspapers. And there was money, lots of it . . . although most of it was settling into fewer and fewer pockets. And there were still those rough, unkept, uncivilized characters who kept wandering through and over these mountains, looking and scratching at every out-cropping, hoping for something, but really not caring too much one way or the other. No matter if all the big discoveries already had been made . . . no matter at all. There just could be another just around that next bend in the canyon . . . or just over that next mountain. Gold, they said, was where you found it, and so was silver.

And so they wandered, carrying everything they needed on their backs, or more often, on the backs of uncomplaining burros or mules. There had been prospectors here before . . . over in the next valley . . . and they'd found it . . . not much, but enough to keep them going. Everybody knew this was silver country and so they continued to peck and dig. There had been others here before . . . many of them. Ranchers had moved into the wide, lush valley nearly 20-years before and there was a heavily-traveled stagecoach road that ran up the Rio Grande from Del Norte, through spectacular Wagon Wheel Gap toward Lake City and Silverton. Nobody paid much attention to the tiny creek flowing from deep in the mountains. There was nothing here, they knew . . . just another stream and just another canyon, and there was a long and often terrifying road ahead of them.

But, there was a cabin up that canyon built by old Haskell Ryder two years before another small prospecting party wandered in . . . a veterann searcher named Nicholas Creede and two companions. And that did it.

Creede tried to keep it quiet . . . what he had found there under a pine-tree on the side of the canyon. It was an out-cropping loaded with silver . . . enough to make him shout "Holy Moses." And he did keep it quiet . . . until a substantial shipment of ore was made the next year. Even then, and as other mines were begun, there wasn't a great deal of excitement anywhere. Maybe a couple of hundred men came in from the other towns and camps . . . and built crude cabins or set up tents. But, there was no great rush in the beginning . . . as there had been to other great strikes in the state. It was a year-and-a-half after Creede made his first strike that miners got together and decided they ought to have a name for their fledgling, squeezed-in, row town. And they named it Creede. But, then, as the mines began to produce more and still more rich veins were found, interest began to pick up around the state . . . and more men began straggling in, some of them bringing their wives. And, of course, where there were women, there had to be something besides tents for them to live in . . . and more and more cabins began to appear and spill down the canyon and out onto the flats along Willow Creek.

Nicholas C. Creede

There were tent saloons, tent dance-halls, tent hotels and tent stores and just plain tents to live in . . . and all were cold when the snows came into that deep gully. But, then, staying warm and comfortable and well-fed wasn't important . . . except at the moment. If a man cared about those things, then he should have stayed in Leadville or Central City or even in that far-too-citified city of Denver . . . or even Colorado Springs . . . where he could curl his fingers around a tea-cup instead of a mug filled with watered-down-red-eye. But, it wouldn't be too bad, they thought, if they could drink that red-eye someplace besides a cold tent . . . say, inside a regular building with

a floor and walls with windows and a roof . . . and a pot-bellied stove. So, buildings of sawn lumber began to take the place of the tents and the log cabins, and the town actually began to look like a town. And the district began to pick up. Creede had sold his Holy Moses mine to a Denver combine headed by Dave Moffat . . . had sold it for 70-thousand-dollars, plus a rather healthy salary, plus a third of anything he found for the company. And he did pretty well; he found that 12-foot-wide lode of silver and copper up on Mammoth Mountain and also the Amethyst which, by itself, poured forth more than two-million-dollars in the first year of operation. Nicholas Creede was fast on his way to becoming a very wealthy man . . . but one with a tragic day ahead . . . but it was 1891 and the world was made of silver, and he owned a good chunk of it and now, after all those years of searching, nothing could go wrong . . . but something did, only six-years later.

But then, the Rio Grande had taken note of the increasing production of the mines at Creede. It had an unproductive branch line to Wagon Wheel Gap; hauled health-seekers to the mineral springs, but lost money on the deal. There was an argument, but the line was run on up the valley and into Creede . . . and paid all its construction costs in only four-months. It was the coming of the railroad that seemed to focus attention on Creede . . . in December 1891. And the dam broke. Suddenly, they came from everywhere . . . grinning and shouting

''And more and more cabins began to appear and spill down the canyon . . . along Willow Creek.''

and yelling, crammed into railroad cars . . . pouring out at the new bonanza . . . each looking for a piece of the action. There hadn't been anything like it for 15-years . . . and 15 years was far too long for a dedicated boom-towner to wait for another boom-town. Some came with picks and shovels; other came with dice and cards, and everybody lived it up. Ten-thousand of them came and squeezed into the tiny area . . . and jostled each other and fought each other and even killed each other . . . and built a town like nobody had ever seen before. Upper Creede spilled down into Jimtown and Jimtown butted into Lower Creede . . . and they spread out on the flats. There were arguments over the name of Jimtown. Depending on whom you talked to, it was Jimtown or New Town or

Creede Railroad Station

Amethyst or Creedmore . . . and even Gin Town, because some said, the only thing a man could get to drink there was watered-down gin that was awful to begin with . . . and in those days, that was very important to a man . . . especially the scores who slept in a cold railroad car, or in a cold tent, or on the cold floor of some cold saloon or dance-hall; it was very important. But a man slept only when he was forced to; there was too much sawing and pounding and shouting and general commotion, night and day; more than 200 carpenters worked round-the-clock and the buildings, false fronts and all, went up quickly . . . and lots that only a few years before weren't worth a plugged Ute were going for 10-thousand-dollars and more. Creede had arrived . . . and the whole nation knew it. But the towns were down here and the mines were up there . . . and just getting to them was a hard-enough job. Getting coal and supplies up to the mine buildings, holding to the side of the near-vertical cliffs for dear life, and getting the ore back down again was next to impossible. So, men called on those bull-headed but impossible-doing animals . . . the burros and the mules. And, as they had done for so many years in so many different places, they did what they were required to do . . . even sometimes almost willingly. They carried heavy loads up the mountains, and heavy loads down the mountains . . . and, again, made men wealthy.

Willow Creek 1890's

And as the mines up there on the sheer cliffs poured their treasure down into the towns in the valley, the boom continued. When night came, Creede's pulse seemed to increase . . . in the glare of endless rows of candles and kerosene lamps . . . and Cy Warman wrote his famous lines . . . it's day all day in the day-time, and there is no night in Creede". A Denver newspaper sent a reporter down to see what was going on . . . and what was going on apparently shocked him . . . for he wrote: "Thirty saloons are in full blast night and day; each saloon has a gambling attachment. The places are thronged at all hours with men in the various stages of drunkeness, and oaths and ribaldry and wantonness, with an occasional scrap, relieve the dreadful evil monotony of jingling glasses and clicking chips. Every species of deviltry can be called into existence at any moment."

Creede 1890's

And Creede had other troubles . . . since, for one thing, it was built astraddle Willow Creek. And Willow Creek could and did get rambunctious at times. But, then, a little water never hurt much . . . if taken in small doses. When the creek jumped its banks and poured through the already-muddy streets, nobody paid a great deal of attention . . . at least not for long. There was too much else going on, too many other things to talk and think about . . . like, for instance, the shennanigans of Soapy Smith, the notorious gambler and bunco artist who actually took over Creede and ran it . . . his

Gunnison Exchange Saloon

way. He was respectful of the legitimate businessmen and he was respectful of everybody else, too . . . as long as they paid him a cut of the take. He brought in a Texas gun-slinger and made him Chief of Police and there was something almost bordering on law and order . . . some of the time. But Soapy and his crew finally ran their string out in Creede, passed through Cripple Creek and wound up in Skagway where Soapy ran into a bullet at the age of 38 . . . a boom-towner right to the very end.

It was the morning of June 5th, 1892 when Creede got its baptism . . . of fire. It started in a saloon and spread rapidly . . . whipped by a breeze down the canyon. And it was a disaster. The heat was held in by the narrow valley slopes and became intense and the flames jumped from one tinder-box building to another. Men ran through the streets shouting and firing their guns, and locomotive whistles were kept blowing . . . to awaken those who were asleep. And people ran in all directions trying to escape the blistering heat and carried out what little they could before the building was engulfed. Before the wind changed, 2½-hours later, most of Creede had been levelled . . . but not one single person had been killed. There was a moment of shock, but even before all the flames were out, Creede . . . being Creede . . . showed its wild side. One reporter wrote: "It was a debauch. Cases of wine, bottles of whiskey, boxes of cigars and other goods were stolen and hundreds were drunk before the flames had half burned down." But, then, citizens armed themselves, guarded the ruins, closed unburned saloons, stripped the looters . . . and the town was quiet again, what was left of it.

Creede fire — June 1892

After the fire, a man named Bob Ford . . . a gambler . . . quickly set up a tent-saloon and opened for business, but he lived just one more day. An unsavory character named Ed O'Kelly strode into the saloon with a double-barreled shotgun . . . and got Ford with both barrels. And a huge crowd quickly gathered out front . . . and just five-minutes after Ford was killed . . . the crowd posed for its photograph. Ford's gambling fraternity friends took him up to the cemetery and gave him a rousing send-off . . . no flowers, no tears . . . but

". . . and just five minutes after Ford was killed . . . the crowd posed for its photograph."

Bob Ford
". . . for he was famous and infamous, in his own time . . ."

plenty of wine and champagne. And today, 76-years later, people still pause to see the grave of Bob Ford . . . for he was famous, and infamous, in his own time . . . as "the dirty little coward who shot Mr. Howard and laid poor Jesse in his grave." Ed O'Kelly, the man who shot the man who shot Jesse James, did 10-years in prison, was paroled, went to Oklahoma where he slugged an officer . . . and was shot dead for it. Ford's body stayed in his grave at Creede only two months until his widow took it back to Cass County, Missouri, for reburial. The place where his saloon stood and where he was killed is marked today with a brass plaque . . . just part of Creede's violent past.

Bob Ford's funeral

After the fire in 1892, Creede rebuilt . . . but the town began to change. The fire seemed to purge the town; free-spending prospectors began to leave, and with them went the saloon-keepers and the gamblers and the ladies, and all those who lived by their wits and schemes on others' money. The mines kept pouring out their silver in the millions . . . nearly four-million dollars in the peak year of 1893. But it was that year that shook all the silver towns . . . the year that Congress passed the Sherman Silver Act and prices plummeted. Only those mines with high-grade could keep producing; the others had to close . . . and hundreds of men who knew only how to dig in hard-rock were without jobs . . . and with families to feed. They paused only briefly, then they, too, began to leave in droves . . . as quickly as they had come. And with them went many of the businessmen whose goods were only gathering dust. And Creede became only a whisper; the fantastic, frantic, shrill and high-living boom had lasted less than two-years . . . and was gone . . . like an echo in the deep canyon above town. It was like a skyrocket . . .bright, brilliant and loud . . . and died as quickly. Those who deserted the district . . . and the many hundreds of others who poured away from the silver towns . . . found another place equally as wild and loud and wonderful . . . a booming gold camp up behind Pike's Peak, a place called Cripple Creek. And so they went . . . and left their stories behind them . . . stories of gun-fighter Bat Masterson who'd left his job

''It's not a very big place . . . . this place called Creede. It never was very big and didn't last very long . . .''

as Deputy Sheriff in Denver and had come to Creede to manage a saloon and gambling hall . . . stories of the day they buried gambler Joe Simmons, up on the hill . . . a bitterly cold day . . . and the coffin clipped out of the wagon and went scooting back down the ice-covered trail . . . but Joe didn't fall out. There were stories of Slanting Annie and Lulu Slain, and Creede Lilly and Rose Vastine and the others. And, of course, there was the story of Nicholas Creede himself, the man who'd started the boom and had become extremely wealthy. He'd left his Indiana home, heart-broken, at 19 . . . because his girl-friend married his brother; had poked around the mountains for nearly 20 hard years before he found what he was looking for at Creede. He took his money and moved to California, but tragedy pursued him. It was only eight years after he'd found the Holy Moses that millionaire William Harvey, alias Nicholas Creede, took his own life . . . because his wife insisted on living with him. That was Creede all right.

Carl Akers' Colorado
was set in 10-point Helios
and printed on 80 lb. Mojave Matte
by Johnson Litho Inc., Loveland, Colo.

Design by Leslie A. Johnston